CURIOUS
Minds

CURIOUS
Minds

40 Hands-on Activities
to Inspire a Love
of Learning

TY KOLSTEDT & DR. AZEEM Z. VASI

Zephyr Press

Chicago

Published by Zephyr Press
An imprint of Chicago Review Press Incorporated
814 North Franklin Street
Chicago, Illinois 60610
ISBN 978-1-61373-150-5

Library of Congress Cataloging-in-Publication Data
Names: Kolstedt, Ty, author. | Vasi, Azeem Z., author.
Title: Curious minds : 40 hands-on activities to inspire a love of learning /
     Ty Kolstedt and Dr. Azeem Z. Vasi.
Description: First edition. | Chicago, Illinois : Zephyr Press, an imprint of
     Chicago Review Press Incorporated, [2015]
Identifiers: LCCN 2015029802 | ISBN 9781613731505
Subjects: LCSH: Activity programs in education. | Motivation in education.
Classification: LCC LB1027.25 .K655 2015 | DDC 371.3--dc23 LC record available at
 http://lccn.loc.gov/2015029802

Cover and interior design and illustrations: Andrew Brozyna, AJB Design, Inc.

Printed in the United States of America
5 4 3 2 1

For Cora, Zara, and Amir

CONTENTS

ACKNOWLEDGMENTS xi

INTRODUCTION 1

 PART I PHYSICS & MATH

Shoot! Mine Didn't Open: The Science of Parachutes...............................4

Is a Penny Saved Really a Penny Earned? Lessons in Investing..............7

Spanning the Ages: The Physics of Bridges 10

The Great Ice Enigma: Conservation of Mass
    and the Science of Volume.. 13

Calorie Tracker: Intake Versus Output... 16

Taking Off! The Science of Flight... 23

Something Borrowed, Something New: How Credit Works................. 27

How Does That Boat Float? Water Displacement
    and Buoyancy 30

 PART II CHEMISTRY

Molecules, Atoms, and Peanut Brittle:
    How Good Chemistry Can Taste 34

Peter Piper Picked a Peck of Cucumbers?
    Food Preservation Then and Now...37

The Silent Buildup: Cholesterol, Fats, and Oil................................ 40

The Original Solar Panel: How Leaves Harness Energy 44

The Bright Side of Decomposition: Plants, Pressure, and Oil 48

Are You a Mosquito Magnet? To Learn and Protect.........................51

PART III LANGUAGE ARTS

Take Shelter, There's a Brainstorm Rolling In!
The Starting Point of Creative Writing.. 56

Marking Its Way Through History: The Story of Ink 59

Wizard of Words: Metaphors and Similes 62

The Sleuth of Truth: A Literary Treasure Hunt............................... 65

안녕하세! World Wise: Languages Around the Globe........................ 68

How to Sign What's on Your Mind: Learning Sign Language................71

PART IV EARTH SCIENCE

Don't Move—You're in Quicksand! 76

Getting the Dirt on Soil Pollution 79

More Than Just a Pretty Taste: Crystals 82

Aahh. . . The Air We Breathe 85

Nothing New Under the Sun: The Beauty of the Water Cycle 88

Hey Fellow, Why's That Pulp Yellow?
The Science of Antique Paper 90

PART V SOCIAL STUDIES

Go West! The American Pioneer 94

Globalization: How the World Is Connected 97

The Songs of the Wind: Native American Religious Tradition........... 100

Democracy! What's Your Vote? 104

Rock the Vote by "Rocking the Boat"? 107

How Much of the Story Are You Getting? Bias in the Media 111

This Land Is My Land, This Land Is Your Land:
The Black Hills Treaty..113

The Fabric of America: Immigration 117

PART VI BIOLOGY

When Nighttime Is the Right Time: Nocturnal Adaptations 122

Caustic Consequences: pH-inding Out About Your Water.................... 125

How the Gills Get Their Fill: Absorbing Oxygen as a Fish..................... 128

Say What? The Science of Sound 132

Fun Guy or Fungi? The World of Yeasts and Molds................................ 137

The Rotten Truth About Your Teeth... 141

ACTIVITIES LIST BY PRIMARY SKILLS FOCUS.. 145

ACKNOWLEDGMENTS

We want to especially thank our agent, MaryAnn Kohl, for everything she has done for us. Her unwavering support, guidance, and belief in us and our project have helped us more than she could possibly know.

INTRODUCTION

"Give the pupils something to do, not something to learn; and the doing is of
such a nature as to demand thinking; learning naturally results."
—John Dewey

While Dewey's words would not seem out of place in a cutting-edge curriculum manual today, the father of the American education system actually wrote them in 1916. Dewey's idea of "learning by doing" forms the bedrock of *Curious Minds* and our philosophy that children learn more when they are actively engaged with the material. Within this book, you will find 40 hands-on learning activities that promote critical thinking and authentic inquiry across a variety of subject areas. Our goal is to turn children into scientists, historians, mathematicians, and writers by getting them excited about gaining new knowledge about the world we live in. This book can be used by parents, teachers, or homeschoolers searching for new ways to get kids motivated about learning. These activities are designed to stimulate young minds, whether they are done in the kitchen or the classroom.

While we have included learning activities encompassing all four core academic areas (math, science, social studies, and language arts), we have also categorized them by specific content focus (physics, biology, chemistry, etc.). The organization of each learning activity is fairly straightforward. Each activity has:

A content and a primary skills focus:

Content Focus:
- Physics/Math
- Chemistry
- Language Arts
- Earth Science
- Social Studies
- Biology

Primary Skills Focus:
- Investigating and Classifying
- Design and Model
- Measuring and Observing
- Interpreting Data
- Historical Inquiry
- Exploring Connections
- Creative Expression

Mission Objective: This section introduces the topic and can include anything from a history of parachutes to an explanation of how oil is formed. This is the background knowledge and "book learning" part of the educational activity.

Learning the Lingo: To become a scientist, historian, or writer one must "speak the language." Learning the Lingo introduces children to key vocabulary terms they will need to know to fully understand the specific learning activity.

Materials: What items are needed to complete the "mission," or activity?

Plan of Attack: This is where things start to get interesting. The Plan of Attack outlines the step-by-step procedural directions of how to *do* the learning activity. In this step, children are transformed into ecologists examining soil pollution, economists analyzing interest rates, and writers creating colorful prose.

Take It to the Max! Once children have learned background information on the topic and have seen it in action, our hope is that we have merely whet their appetites. Take It to the Max! consists of independent extension ideas for children who are interested in delving further into a specific topic.

We thank you for purchasing *Curious Minds* and hope that children in your life find the learning activities engaging, enlightening, and fun!

"I hear and I forget.
I see and I remember.
I do and I understand."
—Confucius

PART I

PHYSICS & MATH

SHOOT! MINE DIDN'T OPEN: THE SCIENCE OF PARACHUTES

Content Focus: Physics
Primary Skills Focus: Design and Model

Mission Objective: Jump into the basics of air resistance with a brief history of parachute design. Then, construct multiple styles of parachutes and test the merits of each design.

Da Vinci's parachute

If you take a feather and pea and drop them from the same height, which one falls faster? The pea, right? One of the reasons this is the case is air resistance. In this mission you will become an expert in air resistance and design your own parachutes.

The idea of the parachute has been around for hundreds of years. While some say the ancient Chinese used a parachute-like device to jump from heights and perform acrobatics, Leonardo Da Vinci created the first known drawings of a modern-style parachute in 1483. His design was a four-sided pyramid made of wood and canvas. In June 2006 Adrian Nicholas glided to the ground safely using a parachute based on a sketch Da Vinci did of his parachute design. The builders of Nicholas's parachute only used materials that would have been available to Da Vinci during his life. Isn't that cool?

Parachutes work because of air resistance. When a parachute is deployed (opened) there is drag, or air resistance, that pushes up the parachute and slows down the jumper. It is the parachute's light weight and large surface area that harness the power of air resistance. It's all about air molecules. A human without a parachute would fall fast because he or she would push through the air molecules very easily (like the pea). Air resistance is generated as the parachute runs into air molecules when hurling toward the Earth (like the feather). The force of all these air molecules pushing against the parachute slows its descent (drop).

Circular parachute

After Da Vinci made his initial drawings in the 15th century, progress on the idea slowed and the parachute did not play a significant role until the early 20th century (or 1900s). Parachutes had lost the rigid frame and were now made of either nylon or silk. From the early 1900s to the 1960s parachutes had a circular design as shown here:

While these parachutes did get the traveler to the ground safely, the jumper didn't have the ability to steer them. The parafoil parachute design created in the 1960s included that improvement. The parafoil design is a rectangular-shaped wing capable of being steered to where its passenger wants to land. Did you know that some competition jumpers can land within inches of a target?

Parafoil parachute

Learning the Lingo

air molecules: The tiny, microscopic building blocks of nitrogen, oxygen, and carbon dioxide that make up the atmosphere around our planet.

descent: The movement down, or lower. In this case it refers to the parachute jumper's fall to the ground.

drag: The air resistance that is created by an object falling. Typically, items with less mass and more surface area create more drag and fall slower.

parafoil: A parachute design developed in the 1960s that gave the jumper greater control and mobility. This is due to the rectangular design and air "pockets" that jumpers can steer with handles, or toggles. This design is still used today.

Materials

- 3 heavy trash bags
- 1 roll of tape
- 1 roll of string
- 50–75 Popsicle sticks
- Wood glue
- 3 plastic shopping bags
- 1 roll of paper towels
- 3 eggs

Plan of Attack

We know the parafoil parachute provides the jumper with the most mobility (the ability to steer), but which design (Da Vinci's, a complete circle, or the parafoil) can land a jumper softest, and therefore safest?

1. Hypothesize (make your best educated guess) as to which design is safest. Why do you think that?

2. Use the trash bags, tape, string, and Popsicle sticks and glue to create three parachutes: a Da Vinci, a circular, and a parafoil. You will use the sticks and glue for the Da Vinci design but for the most part try to use the same amount of material for each parachute. You will want to reinforce the holes in the parachute corners where you tie your strings with small pieces of duct tape. The drag will put

significant pressure on the bag and it may tear without reinforcement.

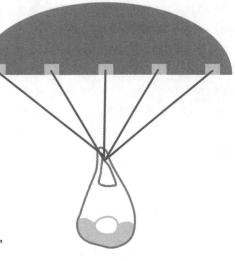

3. Use the plastic shopping bags to make a cradle for an egg to hang under the parachutes. Tie the parachute strings to the plastic shopping bag handle. At the bottom of the bag, use paper towels to cushion the egg.

4. Next, have an adult drop each egg/parachute combination. Try to drop them from an upstairs window, balcony, stairwell, or ladder. Your goal is to drop them from as high as possible to give the parachute the greatest opportunity to "catch" enough air resistance to guide the egg down.

5. What happened? Was your hypothesis correct?

6. Try putting a small hole in the middle of each parachute and see if that helps balance and smooth out the descent. Why might that help?

7. Try experimenting with different-sized parachutes of the same design. What is the relationship between parachute size and speed of descent?

Take It to the Max!

While the goal of the parachute is to slow the jumper down and allow him or her to land where he or she wants, what if you want to feel what it is like to fly? There are action sports enthusiasts who wear a special suit called a *wingsuit*. This is a suit with fabric connecting the arms and legs (think of a flying squirrel). Do some investigating to figure out how these suits work and how these daredevils are actually riding the wind!

Wingsuit parafoil

IS A PENNY SAVED REALLY A PENNY EARNED? LESSONS IN INVESTING

Content Area: Math
Primary Skills Focus: Interpreting Data

Mission Objective: Explore the world of investing and get an introduction to the stock market. "Buy" stock in a company of your choosing and track your "money" over time.

You are about to become an investment wizard as you learn about the stock market and the banking system. Have you ever wondered how the stock market works? Can someone make money by just putting that money in the bank? Can you lose money when you invest it?

It is never too early to learn about savings and investments, and this is your chance to become an investment expert. Next stop, Wall Street!

Learning the Lingo

compound interest: When you have interest added to principal and that new total gains interest as well. Confused yet? Check this out:

Your Savings Account

Principal Amount	$1,000
Interest Per Year	10% (10% of 1,000 is $100)
Amount in Your Account After 1 Year:	$1,100 (1,000 + 100)
Interest for 2nd Year	10% (10% of 1,100 is $110)
Amount in Your Account After 2 Years:	$1,210 (1,100 + 110)

You started with $1,000, and after two years of compound interest you have $1,210.

interest: An excess or bonus on loaned or invested money. Example: if you put money in a savings account the bank actually gives you extra money just for keeping the money in that account. Interest is usually described as a percentage.

principal: The original amount of money described when investing, as in the amount of loan or investment that you start out with. If someone loans you $1,000, that is the principal amount.

shares: A way to represent part ownership in a corporation or other investment. One share is one unit of ownership of whatever you are investing in.

stocks: Certificates that represent the percentage of a company that you own by investing money in that company. These stocks can be bought and sold on something called the stock market. Some people also call these shares.

Materials

- Calculator
- Scrap paper
- A newspaper from the last seven days with a stock market section (found in the business or financial section) or access to the Internet and the page www.google.com/finance

Plan of Attack

Buying and selling stocks is one way to invest money. Stocks each have a unique "ticker symbol," which is a set of letters that represent that company. These ticker symbols help you track the price of stock in the company you have invested in.

Selected Companies and Their Ticker Symbols

Coca-Cola	KO
Google	GOOG
Wal-Mart	WMT
AT&T	T
Ford Motor Co.	F

1. Studying the stock market information you found online or in the paper, find the prices for one share of each of these companies' stock.

2. What would explain the different costs of stock in each of these companies?

3. Pick one of the stocks from this list. Imagine you had $1,000 to invest in stock of your chosen company. How much stock could you buy? (Hint: divide your total amount of money ($1,000) by the price of your chosen stock.)

4. On the first day, write down the number of stock you could buy with your $1,000.

5. At the end of one week, imagine you sell all the shares of stock you bought. Look up the price of stock for your company on day seven and multiply that by the number of shares of stock you own (from step 4).

6. How much money did you end up with? Did you gain money or lose money?

7. Why would someone invest money in the stock market if you could lose it?

8. How much money would you have if you put your initial investment ($1,000) in a savings account that earned 5 percent interest per year after one year? What if you kept your principal and your yearly interest in the account every year; how much would you have after 10 years?

As you can see above, investing can be risky. If you sell a stock for a lower price than you paid for it, you can end up losing money. But, if the company does well you can make money just by owning that small piece of it.

Over the long term, investing your money in an account that pays interest lets you take advantage of compound interest that helps your money grow. After doing these exercises you can see how by putting money in a savings account you can be making money from the compound interest.

So get to it and start investing and saving now!

Take It to the Max!

What are dividends on a company's stock? Do all companies that have stock give out dividends? If you use your dividends to buy more stock, does compound interest help you make more money? Learn about the money-making power of dividends!

SPANNING THE AGES: THE PHYSICS OF BRIDGES

Content Focus: Physics
Primary Skills Focus: Design and Model

Mission Objective: Discover the principles of compression, tension, and bridge construction. Construct multiple bridges using different styles and techniques to test your newfound knowledge.

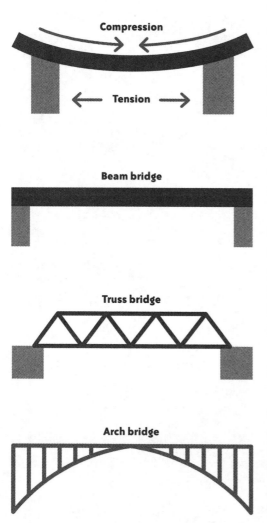

Compression

Tension

Beam bridge

Truss bridge

Arch bridge

What are some structures that were built thousands of years ago and still exist today? You were right if you guessed the Great Wall of China or the Egyptian pyramids. But did you also know that there are other structures that have stood the test of time? In this mission you will take on the role of engineer and learn all about these sturdy marvels: bridges. How do bridges work? What kind of engineering advances made some bridges strong, even thousands of years after they were originally built?

Any bridge that spans a distance has distinct forces acting upon it: compression and tension. Compression refers to the forces acting upon that bridge that push in, or compress, when weight is applied to the bridge. Tension refers to forces that try to stretch, or lengthen out, the bridge when weight is put on the bridge.

This activity will focus on three types of bridges: beam, truss, and arch.

A beam bridge is the most basic type. It consists of a horizontal beam supported by two vertical piers (or abutments). There is a lot of tension and compression acting upon this bridge so the materials that make up the bridge must be very strong. The longer the beam bridge, the weaker it becomes. You rarely see a beam bridge over 250 feet long.

A truss bridge is a more complicated type of bridge made out of interconnected triangles to increase the strength of the bridge. The trusses transfer the compression and tension from one point over the entire span of the bridge.

In a truss bridge the load (the compression and tension) is not just on one beam (like the beam bridge) but is shared between the top beam, bottom beam, and supporting triangles. Because the beams and triangles are connected, when the weight of the load is applied to the bridge, the weight burden is spread out and the entire bridge helps support the load.

An arch bridge is a semi-circle connected to supports (or abutments) on each side. This can be a very strong bridge because the compression is pushed outward toward the abutments so the beam does not have to support the whole load of the bridge.

Learning the Lingo

abutments: The foundation points on each side of a bridge that support its weight.

compression: The act of pressing or squeezing together. This happens on every bridge when weight is applied.

span: The portion of the bridge between its abutments, or supports.

tension: The act of stretching or pulling apart. This happens on every bridge when weight is applied.

truss: A rigid triangular framework used to increase the strength of a bridge by dividing the tension and compression among multiple supports.

Materials

- 2 chairs
- 500+ popsicle sticks (available at craft or hobby supply stores)
- Wood glue
- 5–10 spring-tight binder clips or clothespins
- String
- Bucket of water

Plan of Attack

There are a couple different ways to do this activity. If you are alone, take option 1. If you are doing this activity with someone, take option 2. First, hypothesize on which bridge type (beam, truss, or arch) will hold the most weight. Why?

OPTION 1

Build all three types of bridges and test out which one will hold the most weight. Note: You may want to do this activity outside as the floor may get wet.

1. First take your chairs, put the seat sections facing each other, and separate them about one foot apart. This will be how far your bridges need to span.

2. Next, build all three types of bridges using the popsicle sticks and glue. Use the binder clips to hold the sticks together while the glue is drying. Be creative with this and have fun. Try to build the strongest beam, truss, and arch bridges you can. For the arch bridges you may have to bend (or break) the popsicle sticks and glue them back together to form the arch.

3. To test out the strength of each, hang the bucket beneath each bridge as it spans the chairs. Add water, one cup at a time, until each bridge fails. The bridge that can hold the most water wins.

OPTION 2

In this option, you and a partner compete to see who can build the stronger bridge. You may choose to build any of the bridges (beam, truss, or arch) depending on which you feel you can build to be the strongest. Follow the same steps listed in Option 1. Whoever builds the bridge that can hold the most water wins.

Take It to the Max!

The technology used to make these bridges strong can be found in many different structures. For example, the construction of a house's roof involves trusses because of their strength. The Roman Coliseum still stands (almost 2,000 years later) because of the vaulted arches that made the walls extremely strong while cutting down on weight.

As you travel, pay attention to what kinds of bridges you cross. Try to notice the other uses for the beam, truss, and arch designs in architecture all around you. Also, be on the lookout for another kind of bridge design, suspension. Do some research (either on the Internet or at the library) and discover why suspension bridges may be superior to all others.

THE GREAT ICE ENIGMA: CONSERVATION OF MASS AND THE SCIENCE OF VOLUME

Content Area: Physics
Primary Skills Focus: Measuring and Observing

Mission Objective: Learn the principles of conservation of mass and matter using ice and water to get a hands-on look at these principles in action.

You are about to prove some basics principles of science that your eyes may not even believe! Have you ever watched a glass full of ice melt into water? What happens when the ice melts? It doesn't seem to make sense: the glass that was full of ice is now only half full of water.

In this mission you will learn what is happening to the mass of an object by observing what happens when the ice melts to form water. You will master a basic principle of science that will start off your quest to be the next Albert Einstein or Marie Curie. Prepare to master the conservation of mass.

Learning the Lingo

conservation of mass: A principle of science that shows that mass can't be created or destroyed but it can be rearranged in different forms and different particles when you are in a closed, or isolated, system. (An example of a closed system is the plastic glass you will use in the activity to follow.)

conservation of matter: Don't let the different names confuse you, mass and matter are the same thing. So, in physics, conservation of matter is the exact same thing as conservation of mass.

mass: Simply put, mass is how much of an object there is; the mass of an object can be weighed using different units, like pounds or kilograms.

metric system: A measurement system created in France in 1791. This system of measurements is used all over the world and measures distances in the form of meters and volumes in the form of liters.

United States Customary System: A measurement system, also called *English Units*, that is used widely in the United States for measuring. Some examples are miles, inches, pints, and gallons. You can convert metric units to English units if you know the calculations.

volume: The amount of space that an object takes up. If you fill up a 20-milliliter container with sand, the volume of the sand is 20 milliliters.

Materials

- Kitchen or food weighing scale
- Clear plastic cup
- Ice
- Paper and writing utensil
- Masking tape
- Ruler

Plan of Attack

Conservation of mass is an interesting scientific principle that shows that you can neither create nor destroy matter. But what does that really mean, and where can you see that in your own life? You are about to find out.

Different objects around you have a different mass, or amount of the object, that can be calculated by weight. In the United States, the units we often use to measure the mass of objects are pounds and ounces. But the mass of an object doesn't dictate the amount of space it takes up, or volume. A two-liter bottle of soda is heavier than your bedroom pillow even though the pillow takes up more space. This is because the mass of the soda is more, even though it has a smaller volume. It sounds easy, but it can get tricky. Does a cup full of ice have the same mass, or weight, before it melts as it will after the ice becomes water? What is the volume of the ice compared to the volume of water?

You are about to find out the answer to these questions and more.

1. Fill your cup to the top with ice and weigh it on the scale. Note the weight and write it down.

2. Wait till the ice melts completely.

3. Take the cup that has the water from the melted ice and weigh it again on the scale. Note the weight and write it down.

4. Place a piece of tape on the side of the cup, running from the bottom of the cup to the top line of the water, to mark what level the water has reached.

5. Now carefully place the cup into your freezer. Remove it when the water is completely frozen.

6. Use your ruler to measure the distance between the top line of the tape and the top line of the ice. Also, weigh cup again and record your findings.

Brain Buster Questions

1. Was the weight of the glass with ice and with the melted ice (water) the same or different?

2.   How do you explain your results?

3.   What took up more space in the glass, the water or the water after it was frozen?

4.   Is it the mass that has changed, or the volume?

EXPLANATION

The ice and the water in the first three steps have the same mass because of the principle of conservation of mass. Nothing was created or destroyed; it just changed form—from water to ice—so the weight stayed the same. The mass didn't change but the volume did. Water has a unique feature that you proved in this experiment: it takes up more volume when frozen than when liquid. Most matter takes up less volume when frozen.

You can try the activity as many times as needed so you can clearly understand the principles you have learned above. With a little time you will have mastered the principles of conservation of mass. Are you ready to tackle the next challenge?

Take It to the Max!

Did you know that if you were standing on the moon the mass of your body would be the same as on Earth but your weight would be different? A child that weighs 100 pounds on Earth would weigh only 16.6 pounds on the moon. Learn about what principle of physics could account for the difference in body weight between the Earth and moon.

CALORIE TRACKER: INTAKE VERSUS OUTPUT

Content Focus: Math
Primary Skill Focus: Interpreting Data

Mission Objective: Eat your way through the basics of caloric intake versus output and what that means for the human body. Track your own intake/output and come to conclusions about your own lifestyle choices.

Here's a crazy fact for you: the only energy that ever gets added to the cycle of life on Earth comes from the sun (as you will see in The Original Solar Panel on page 44). Plants turn the energy in the sun's rays into "food" by a process called *photosynthesis*. No new energy is ever produced in our universe; it's just recycled over and over again in new and different ways. For example, a plant takes in sunlight and uses that sunlight to grow into a big, strong corn plant. A farmer cuts down the corn and feeds it to a pig. The energy that was in the corn (originally from the sun) is now in the pig. The pig is then processed and turned into ham that we eat, and the energy from the pig helps us grow strong and do our daily activities. When we die, if we are buried our bodies go back into the Earth, and that gives energy and nutrients to the soil to grow more food for other plants and animals.

A *calorie* is the unit of measure of how much of this energy is in our food. The scientific definition for a calorie is the amount of energy it takes to heat one gram of water by one degree Celsius. You hear a lot about calories these days. You take in calories when you eat and you burn calories through exercise and your daily activities. The simple truth is that you'll gain weight if you take in (or eat) more calories than you burn. On the other hand, you'll lose weight if you burn more calories than you consume. In this activity you will track your calorie intake and output over the course of three days.

Learning the Lingo
calorie: Commonly used unit for measuring amounts of food energy; one calorie is the amount of energy required to heat one gram of water by one degree Celsius.
intake: The process of taking in or consuming food.
output: Total amount of energy used (measured in calories) by doing certain activities.

Materials
  • Paper and writing utensil

Plan of Attack

On the following pages you will find a list of commonly found foods and how many calories they contain. Remember, not everything you eat will be on this list. Most of the time you can look at the side of the box or wrapper to see how many calories you are consuming. Just remember to pay attention to the portion size. For example, a popular macaroni and cheese brand states that each portion is one cup and contains 410 calories. If you end up eating one and a half cups, you would then multiply the 410 by 1.5 to get a caloric intake of 615 for that portion of the meal.

You will also find a list of how many calories are burned doing everyday activities.

Food	Serving Size	Calories
Apple	1	81
Apple juice	3/4 cup	87
Avocado	1/2 cup	121
Bacon	1 slice	36
Bagel	1	200
Baked Beans	1/2 cup	130
Banana	1	96
Beef jerky	1 strip	67
Beef stew	1 cup	161
Beef stroganoff	1 cup	350
Blackberries	1/2 cup	37
Blueberries	1/2 cup	41
Bologna	1 oz.	70
Bread (wheat or white)	Diet: 1 slice	40
	Regular: 1 slice	70
Broccoli	1/2 cup	58
Brownie	1	350
Brussels sprouts	1/2 cup	33
Bun, hamburger	1	140
Bun, hot dog	1	140
Burrito	1	250–450 (depending on size and ingredients)
Butter	1 tbsp.	100
Cake	1 pc.	550
Calzone, 4"	1	100
Carrots	1/2 cup	35
Cauliflower	1/2 cup	17

Food	Serving Size	Calories
Celery	1/2 cup	13
Cereal/oatmeal	1 cup	56–210 (depending on type)
Cheese	Reduced fat: 1 slice	55
	Regular: 1 slice	105
Cheese cake	1 slice	300
Cherries	1/2 cup	52
Chicken	1 oz.	50
Chicken breast	Baked/boiled	200
	Batter/fried	400
Chicken casserole	1 cup	240
Chicken drumstick	Baked/boiled	100
	Batter/fried	200
Chicken thigh	Baked/fried	150
	Batter/fried	300
Chicken/veggie stir fry	1/2 cup	167
Chili	1 cup	225
Chimichanga	1	350
Chocolate pudding	1 cup	150
Club sandwich	1	481
Cocoa (hot chocolate)	1 cup	150
Coleslaw	1/2 cup	175
Corn	1/2 cup	66
	On the cob	112
Corn dog	1	341
Cottage cheese	1/2 cup	90
Cupcake	1	130
Donut	1	250
Egg	Fried: 1	83
	Scrambled: 1	99
	Boiled: 1	66
Egg roll	1	160
Egg salad	1/2 cup	180
Enchilada	1	180
Fajita	1	430
Fettucini alfredo	1 cup	330
Fish	3 oz.	100–145

Food	Serving Size	Calories
French fries	1/2 cup	75
French toast	1 piece	127
Fruit, canned	1/2 cup	100
Green bean casserole	1/2 cup	190
Grilled cheese sandwich	1	300
Ground beef	3 oz.	250
Guacamole	1/4 cup	93
Ham	3 oz.	175
Ham and cheese sandwhich	1	377
Hamburger	No cheese	352
	With cheese	458
Hash browns	1/2 cup	220
Hot dog	No bun	140
	With bun	250–500 (depending on type, length, and condiments)
Hummus	1/4 cup	225
Lasagna	3" square	338
Lemonade	1 cup	92
Macaroni and cheese	1 cup	450
Macaroni salad	1/2 cup	150
Margarine	1 tsp.	30
Meatball (beef)	1	77
Meatloaf	1 slice	200
Melon (cantaloupe, honeydew, etc.)	1 cup	60
Milk (2%)	1 cup	121
Mixed veggies	1/2 cup	19
Muffin, blueberry	1	167
Muffin, English	1	134
Mushrooms	1/2 cup	9
Nachos	1 cup	325
Noodles	1/2 cup	100
Omelet (2 eggs)	No cheese	175
	With cheese	230
Onion rings	1/2 cup	150
Onions (raw)	1/2 cup	30

Food	Serving Size	Calories
Orange juice	3/4 cup	84
Pancakes	1	66
Pastrami	1 oz.	70
Peanut butter	1 tbsp.	96
Pear	1	98
Peas	1/2 cup	62
Peas and carrots	1/2 cup	38
Peppers (red or green)	1/2 cup	19
Pickle	1	5
Pie	1 slice	400
Pizza	1 slice	225
Popcorn	Without butter: 3 cups	92
	With butter: 3 cups	244
Pork chop	3 oz.	200
Pot pie	1	314
Potato chips	1 chip	11
Potatoes	Baked: 1	157
	Hash browned: 1/2 cup	220
	Mashed: 1/2 cup	120
	Scalloped: 1/2 cup	120
Pretzels	1 oz.	85
Ravioli	1 cup	414
Refried beans	1 cup	119
Reuben sandwich	1	554
Ribs	1 piece	139
Rice	1/2 cup	100
Roast beef	3 oz.	170
Roast beef sandwhich	1	344
Roasts (beef)	3 oz.	250
Roll (dinner)	1	130
Sausage	Breakfast link: 1	48
	Chorizo link: 1	220
	Italian link: 1	209
Sesame chicken	1 cup	298
Shrimp	3 oz.	100
Soft drinks	1 can	152

Food	Serving Size	Calories
Spaghetti sauce	1 cup	150
Spinach	1/2 cup	40
Sports drink (Gatorade, etc.)	8 oz.	60
Steak	3 oz.	200
Strawberries	1/2 cup	23
Sub sandwich (cold cut)	6" sandwich: 1	425
Sugar	1 tsp.	16
Sweet potatoes	1/2 cup	134
Sweet sour chicken/pork	1 cup	540
Taco	1	150
Taco salad	1 cup	320
Tamale	1	100
Teriyaki beef/chicken	1 cup	350
Tofu	1/2 cup	75
Tortilla	Corn: 1	100
	Flour: 1	200
Tortilla chip	1 cup	100
Tuna	3 oz.	168
Turkey	3 oz.	160
Waffle	1	150
Yogurt	1 cup	175

*caloric information taken from US Department of Health and Human Services

Keep track of your calorie intake versus output for the next three days to figure out whether you burn as many calories as you are taking in. If you are taking in more than you are burning, you may want to have a conversation with your parents or guardian about eating and activity habits to try to balance these two factors out. Eating too much can lead to weight gain, which can lead to all kinds of diseases and physical problems. On the other hand, maintaining a balance of eating and activity can lead to a healthy life.

Now study the next table, below, which shows the number of calories burned per minute for various activities.

Calories Burned per Hour
for Various Activities

Activity	Calories Burned / hour
Active sports (basketball, tennis, soccer, etc.)	440
Aerobics	480
Biking	290
Bowling	300
Dancing	330
Golf	430
Heavy yard work	440
Hiking	370
Housework	180
Light gardening	330
Mowing the lawn	510
Raking leaves	360
Resting/sleeping	50
Running/jogging	590
Shoveling snow	510
Swimming	510
Walking	280
Weight training (heavy)	440
Weight training (light)	220

Keep track of your daily activities for the next three days to determine how many calories you burn each day. Estimated calories burned are based on engaging in each activity for one hour. So, if you do the activity for half an hour, just divide the calories burned by 2. If you do the activity for 15 minutes, divide the calories by 4 to figure out how many calories you just burned.

FUN FACT: Your body is always burning calories (even right now as you read this!). It takes energy to pump your heart, digest your food, breathe, and so on. Be sure to include resting/sleeping into your calorie calculations.

Finally, compare the results of calories consumed versus calories burned over the last three days. Again, your goal should be a healthy balance.

Take It to the Max!

Next time you go to a restaurant, ask to see the nutritional information on all their food; most restaurants will have it available. Fast food restaurants (McDonald's, Wendy's, Taco Bell, and the like) will have the nutritional information available on their websites as well. You might be surprised how much activity you will have to do to burn off that cheeseburger or cheesy smothered burrito.

TAKING OFF! THE SCIENCE OF FLIGHT

Content Area: Physics
Primary Skills Focus: Design and Model

Mission Objective: Soar into an understanding of flight basics such as thrust and pressure and then see these principles in action in the construction of your own planes.

You are about to become a king or a queen of the high skies. In this mission you will see the power of flight come to life by learning about some simple physics. Have you ever wondered how airplanes, which are really heavy, stay up in the sky? Why don't they just fall to the ground like we do when we jump up into the air? Why don't airplanes have to flap their wings like birds to fly?

You don't have to be a pilot to learn about and love flying. Next stop, the friendly skies!

Learning the Lingo

aerodynamics: A branch, or part, of physics that studies the motion and change of air as it comes in contact with a moving object. An example is how air flow changes when it comes in contact with the wings of a plane.

Bernoulli's principle: A principle of physics that tells you that when the speed of the air increases, the pressure that the air exerts, or applies, is lower. You will see how this principle helps planes fly.

Orville and Wilbur Wright: Brothers from Dayton, Ohio, who are considered by many to be the inventors and builders of the first successful airplane. The Wright brothers owned a bicycle store and when they weren't working with the bicycles, they did a lot of testing on aerodynamics in their workshop.

pressure: An effect that happens when force is applied to a surface. When the wind is blowing hard and it hits your face, that is the pressure of the wind on your skin. At certain times the amount of pressure can be so high that it is able to move large objects.

thrust: A force that goes in the forward direction from a jet or rocket engine as a reaction to high-speed ejection of gas, or exhaust, behind it. If you see a jet engine with high exhaust coming out the back, this is actually a force pushing the jet forward.

Materials

- 8.5 inch x 11 inch paper (heavier inkjet printer paper works well, regular notebook paper may be too lightweight)

Plan of Attack

When you look up into the sky and see an airplane flying over your head, do you ever wonder how it is staying up in the air? Think about how heavy the plane is with all the metal it is made of, the people inside of it, and even all the luggage it carries. It almost seems impossible that it could glide easily through the air.

In the early 1900s Orville and Wilbur Wright, brothers from Ohio, had a dream of showing that it *is* possible. At that point in our history, there was no such thing as an airplane, but Orville and Wilbur believed that it would be possible to build an aircraft that was heavier than air that could carry and be controlled by humans. The Wright brothers looked up in the sky and noticed that when birds fly, they change the angle of the ends of their wings to turn left and right. Maybe even more important, the Wright brothers did aerodynamic testing in their workshop and used the ideas of thrust, air pressure, and force to help in their designs.

You might be thinking, *All this talk of aerodynamics and physics is too complicated for me to understand.* Well, it's not! Let's break it down to make it a little simpler. The wings on an airplane provide a surface for air to move against when the plane is moving forward. The wings are specially designed so the top part is curved and the bottom part is not as curved. The air moves easier and faster over the curved top of the wing than the air underneath the wing. As we know from Bernoulli's principle, the air that moves faster across the wing puts less pressure on the wing (slower air has more pressure on the wing). So there is less pressure above the wing than below the wing. This pushes the wings up, and with them the plane, helping it off the ground.

When the plane is going fast enough and the angle of the wing changes, tilting up, it makes even more pressure under the wing, helping it lift even higher. These principles keep the plane in the air flying even though it is heavier than the air around it.

Bernoulli's principle. Illustration redrawn with permission from original source
© 2003 Geoffrey Hill, TeachEngineering.org

Now that you know about how airplanes stay up in the air, it is your turn to try to master flying through the air by building your own planes. Paper airplanes! Use the directions here to follow in the footsteps of the Wright brothers and build your own unique aircraft.

1.   Lay the sheet of paper in front of you vertically. Fold in the top corners as shown.

2.   Fold the top edges inward again so the edges meet in the middle of the paper.

3.   Fold in half lengthwise.

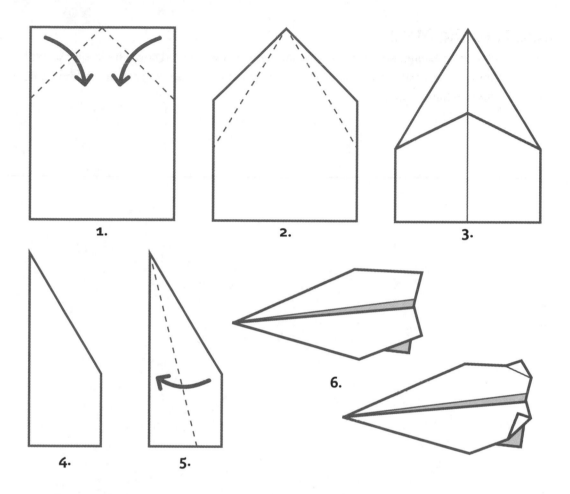

1.   2.   3.

4.   5.

6.

4. Fold the wings down in half lengthwise so that the edge of the paper lines up with the middle crease as shown.

5. Fold up the corners of the wings.

6. Test out your paper airplane. Can you change how well it flies by changing the angle of the wings? Try folding the paper airplane in various ways to see if this changes the angle.

Throw the paper airplane harder. Does it fly longer or higher? Throw the airplane from higher up. Does it fly longer or higher? Make changes based on what you have learned that may make an even better paper airplane design.

Using your paper airplane model, you can see that when you throw the plane you are generating the necessary thrust or force to move it. With force pushing your plane forward, the concepts of air pressure and Bernoulli's principle keep your plane in the air. Be creative and try your different designs to become the ace of aerodynamics.

Take It to the Max!

Now that you have mastered how airplanes fly, have you ever wondered how a helicopter works? Is it the same thing as an airplane? Why doesn't it need wings to fly? See if you can unlock the mystery behind the flight of helicopters.

SOMETHING BORROWED, SOMETHING NEW: HOW CREDIT WORKS

Content Focus: Math
Primary Skills Focus: Interpreting Data

Mission Objective: Charge into the fundamentals of credit and the math behind credit cards. Track purchases and figure out how much you will pay using credit versus saving up to make the purchases outright.

Most adults use credit throughout their lives. When you use credit you borrow money from someone to buy something you need or want (like a house or a car). You must then repay the money to the lender (person or company you borrowed from) plus a little extra called *interest*. This interest, or extra money you pay back, is how lenders make their money. Borrowing money can be a great thing because most of us don't have tens or hundreds of thousands of dollars to buy a house. We take out home loans and pay off a little every month over the course of many years. The same is true for most cars; many people finance (or borrow money to purchase) them and pay the car or truck off over time.

You may have seen your parents use credit cards to purchase everyday items. Using a credit card allows a person to finance smaller items a little bit at a time. This can allow people to track their spending and budget payments on a schedule that works best with their paychecks. However, it can be easy to borrow more than can be paid back before interest charges start to add up. In this activity you are going to track and add up all of your family's spending for a week. You are then going to figure out how much it would've cost your family if they used a credit card to pay for everything.

Learning the Lingo

APR (Annual Percentage Rate): The percentage of the principal you will be charged to borrow the money.

finance: The borrowing of money to purchase something.

interest: A fixed charge or fee for borrowing money.

lender: The person, company, or institution that lends money to an individual.

principal: The original amount of money borrowed, excluding interest.

Materials

- Paper and writing utensil

Plan of Attack

Most credit card companies charge interest based on how much debt you are carrying, on average, throughout the month. They call this your average daily balance. To make the math easy, let's say that you usually charge $1,000 per month on your credit card and that was your average daily balance. Now we need to know our annual percentage rate, or APR. We are going to pretend that our credit card has an APR of 15 percent. Since it is 15 percent for the whole year we need to divide 15 percent by 12 (number of months in the year) to get a 1.25 percent monthly interest rate. We then take our average balance, $1,000, and multiply it by 0.0125 (that's the percentage put in decimal form) to get an interest payment of $12.50 for the month. That means we are paying the credit card company $12.50 to borrow their money for the month.

EQUATION: $1,000 (average daily balance) x 0.0125 (monthly interest rate) = $12.50 (interest payment due)

Paying an extra $12.50 on $1,000 doesn't really sound that bad, right? How people get into trouble is if they don't pay off their balance every month. If you continued spending $1,000 per month and just made the interest payment for six months and didn't pay the principal (the actual money you borrowed), your debt would grow to over $6,000. The interest payment on $6,000 at 15 percent APR would be $75. That's $75 per month just in interest!

EQUATION: $6,000 (average daily balance) x 0.0125 (monthly interest rate) = $75 (interest payment due)

Also, if you miss a payment your rate can go up to 35 percent. If you had a $6,000 balance on your credit card and missed a payment, your interest payment alone could go up to $174 per month! It's easy to see how credit card fees can really add up.

You will track all family spending for one week. You will need to be consistent and talk to your family every night and add up the cost of everything each person purchased (food, gas, household items, etc.). We will pretend that you purchased everything using a credit card with a 15 percent interest rate. Because a 15 percent annual interest rate equals a 1.25 percent monthly rate, you will multiply the family purchases by 0.0125 to see what the interest payments would be on your family purchases if they had used credit to buy everything.

EQUATION: _____ (total purchases) x 0.0125 (monthly interest rate) = _____ (interest payment due)

Now, pretend your family missed a payment and the interest rate shot up to 35 percent. Multiply your purchases by 0.0291 (the monthly interest rate based on a 35 percent APR) to see how important it is to make your payments on time.

EQUATION: _____ (total purchases) x 0.0291 (monthly interest rate) = _____ (interest payment due)

Take It to the Max!

Now you know how credit card companies make their money. While high interest payments are good for the credit card companies, they can be very hard for the people who have to pay them. Try to find credit card offers and commercials in the world around you. Often times they'll offer something, like a magazine subscription or a tote bag, if you apply for a card. What they don't tell you is that if you're not careful, you could wind up paying thousands of dollars in interest when all you got was a $10 subscription or tote bag. It's very important to make sure you understand all terms before signing up for any loan or credit card because, as we have explored, you may be responsible for years of unneeded payments if you consistently choose to "put it on the plastic." You now know enough about credit cards to make wise choices about credit when you get older.

HOW DOES THAT BOAT FLOAT? WATER DISPLACEMENT AND BUOYANCY

Content Focus: Physics
Primary Skills Focus: Design and Model

Mission Objective: After learning basic principles of water displacement and buoyancy you will then test your skills by creating multiple boat hulls using common household products.

Have you ever wondered how an aircraft carrier or a huge cruise ship could possibly float in the ocean? Well, the answer lies in two concepts: buoyancy and water displacement. People have been thinking about these concepts for thousands of years. A famous Greek thinker named Archimedes came up with the idea of water displacement in the third century bce. He noticed that the water in his bath rose every time he got in. Since no two objects can occupy the same space at the same time, his body was *displacing*, or moving, the water exactly the same amount every time. Because our bodies weigh more than the water we push away, or displace, we sink to the bottom of the tub. An object will float if it is lighter than the water it displaces.

Wait, how can this be? How can a person weigh much less than a battleship and yet sink into a tub while a ship floats on the water? The answer lies in the shape of the vessel. When metal is formed into a hull (the bottom of a ship) it creates a metal shell filled with air that is lighter than the water the ship is displacing. As the surface area of a hull increases, it displaces more water and can therefore more easily float.

Another concept that will help us understand why ships float is buoyancy. Buoyancy is the force acting on an object in fluid that forces the object to float up. An object will float (due to buoyancy) if it is either less dense than the water or shaped right (like the hull of a boat). Think about it like this: If you go into a swimming pool and curl up into a ball, you will probably sink. If you lie back and spread your arms and legs, you will most likely float. Why? When you are curled up, less water is pushing against you, making you less buoyant. When you are spread out on top of the water there is more water pushing against you and you are therefore more buoyant. The same is true for the design of a boat. Huge aircraft carriers weigh hundreds of thousands of pounds. If all that metal was smashed together into a ball it would undoubtedly sink to the bottom of the ocean. But, because they shape the hull to spread the weight of the ship out over an increased surface area, the water displacement is spread out over a larger area, which pushes the ship up and increases its buoyancy.

Learning the Lingo

buoyancy: The force that makes an object float on the surface of a liquid as opposed to sink to the bottom. Factors like weight and surface area influence an object's buoyancy.

hull: The frame or body of a ship. The size and shape of a boat's hull influence its buoyancy.

surface area: The exposed area of an object, in this case the bottom of the boat or ship. If weight stays the same, increased surface area will increase buoyancy.

water displacement: The volume of fluid displaced, or moved, by a floating or submerged object.

Materials

For boat

- 4 pieces thick, cardstock paper
- 1 roll duct/electric tape
- aluminum foil

To complete activity

- bathtub
- several handfuls of pennies or other objects that all have the same size and weight (such as beads, marbles, or popcorn kernels)

Plan of Attack

You are going to experiment with different boat designs to determine what kind of design is most buoyant.

1. First hypothesize (make your best educated guess) as to which kind of hull (flat bottom or round bottom) would be most buoyant. Why?

2. Be creative and create a few different boats using the listed materials. Be sure to use the same materials for each boat so that the comparisons will be accurate. No matter how you make your boats, always make sure you waterproof the inside and outside of the hull by wrapping it in aluminum foil and sealing the seams with tape so no water gets in. Make one wide with a flat-bottom hull and another thin with a curved hull that almost makes a V at the bottom.

3. Next, fill up your bathtub about halfway. Put each boat in the water. You may have to manipulate the design of your boats to make them seaworthy. Start counting pennies (or other objects) as you slowly fill up each boat. The boat that stays afloat longest had the most buoyancy. Why? Did this match your prediction? Is there a relationship between the size of the hull (bottom of boat) and the amount of weight it can handle?

Flat bottom and curved boat hulls

Take It to the Max!

We've talked a lot about the size and shape of a ship, but what about the material it is made of? Did you know that until about 150 years ago all ships were made of wood? Why do you think they changed to metal? Why had this not been done before? See if you can figure out what factors led to the creation of the ironclads of the Civil War.

PART II

CHEMISTRY

MOLECULES, ATOMS, AND PEANUT BRITTLE: HOW GOOD CHEMISTRY CAN TASTE

Content Area: Chemistry
Primary Skills Focus: Exploring Connections

Mission Objective: Chew on some of the physics behind molecules, atoms, and matter and observe the transformation between states of matter while making peanut brittle.

You are about to see with your own eyes a world that is all around us but is so tiny that we forget it's even there. Forget those big fancy machines and magnifying glasses, you are about to enter the microscopic world of atoms and molecules in a big and tasty way.

See how atoms, molecules, matter, and heat all take part in making some simple ingredients turn into a hard, tasty, crunchy, peanut-y dessert.

Learning the Lingo

atoms: The smallest little piece of something that can exist alone. If you could break up the air into tiny microscopic pieces, eventually the last piece would be an atom. You can't see an atom with just your eyes, but they are there.

bonds: So what keeps these atoms together to form a molecule? Bonds. Bonds are like invisible small rubber bands that keep atoms close to each other to form a molecule. The even cooler part is that the invisible bonds "stick" different atoms together in different ways.

heat: When the temperature goes up or down, the bonds holding your atoms together can change. These changes can make the way things look change. Things can get harder, softer, and even wetter. Remember what happens when you add a little heat to your ice cubes—they turn to water. You just watched some bonds changing!

matter: All the stuff around you. Matter is a word that scientists use to describe everything that is around you, everything that takes up space. You are made up of matter. Your dog, your TV, and even the air is matter. Matter is everywhere.

molecules: What makes up all this matter? Matter is made up of molecules, and molecules are just atoms that are put together in a special way. Molecules are just a *little* bit bigger than atoms because they are made up of at least two atoms. So why are molecules important? Well, depending on which atoms, and how many atoms, are put together in each molecule, you get different types of matter. That is why an orange looks different than an apple.

Materials

- ½ cup sugar
- ½ cup raw peanuts
- ¼ cup light corn syrup
- Generous pinch of salt
- ½ tablespoon butter
- ½ teaspoon vanilla
- ½ teaspoon baking soda
- Wooden spoon
- Thick-bottomed pot with handle
- Oven mitts
- Pregreased (using small amount of additional butter) baking sheet/pan

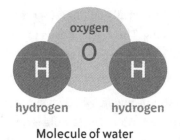

Molecule of water

✳ ***Very Important!*** *Because this mission involves making hot items using the stove or microwave, you need to have a parent or responsible adult do this activity with you. Of course, do not participate in this part of the activity if you have a peanut allergy.*

Plan of Attack

At this point you know quite a bit about atoms, molecules, bonds, and matter. But what do any of these things have to do with cooking a peanut brittle treat? Remember that matter is the "stuff" that is all around you, including the food you eat.

Look again at the ingredients you have gathered. Each ingredient is matter made up of millions of atoms that are bonded together. All of these molecules have different characteristics that make each object of matter, or in this case, each ingredient, different. With different molecules these separate ingredients can look, feel, and taste different.

So how exactly do these ingredients come together to make peanut brittle? This is the magic of chemistry. When matter is exposed to enough heat it can change the molecules of its structure, breaking and reforming bonds. The heat from your stove can change some of the individual ingredients in your recipe to form one whole different type of matter. As you will see in the recipe in this chapter, the bonds within the sugar, salt, and butter will get heated up. These bonds will break and combine together to form a new piece of matter—peanut brittle.

You will notice that after the sugar and corn syrup get heated up they will look totally different, from white powder and syrup to hard brown candy. The chemical bonds between the molecules are broken, and they reform to make a different substance. Some of the other ingredients, like the peanuts, don't change their structure with the heat and will look the same. In this way, making your peanut brittle treat is chemistry in action.

1. Make sure all your ingredients are ready and measured prior to the start of cooking. This recipe needs to be made quickly and you don't have time to measure between steps. Exact times are not given as every stove has different heats, but this whole process will take approximately 9 minutes.

2. Combine sugar, light corn syrup, raw peanuts, and salt in a heavy-bottomed pot with a handle. The handle is important as the final contents will still be hot when they need to be poured later in the recipe.

3. Place your pot on the stove on medium-high heat and stir until the sugar has dissolved.

4. Once dissolved, turn the heat down to medium and let the mixture cook, stirring every few seconds and keeping a close eye on it.

5. The mixture will start turning light brown. At this point start stirring continuously until the mixture is medium brown in color; be careful not to let the mixture burn. (If you are concerned about burning, you can turn the heat down after the mixture becomes light brown in color.)

6. After the medium brown color is reached, use your oven mitts to take the pot off the stove, and then add baking soda, vanilla, and butter.

7. Stir vigorously and immediately pour the mixture onto the buttered baking sheet. With your wooden spoon, spread the mixture out on the buttered baking sheet to form a thin layer.

8. Let the peanut brittle rest until it hardens. This will happen as soon as the brittle starts to cool (typically 30 minutes or longer). Break into pieces and enjoy.

Take It to the Max!

Is an atom too small to split? Has anyone ever tried to split an atom? See if you can unlock the mystery of splitting atoms.

PETER PIPER PICKED A PECK OF CUCUMBERS? FOOD PRESERVATION THEN AND NOW

Content Focus: Chemistry
Primary Skills Focus: Measuring and Observing

Mission Objective: Examine the science and history behind food preservation. Then, make a delicious dish using some of these techniques.

Next time you go into the supermarket, go to the meat and seafood departments and try to find out how many of the different types of fish, poultry (turkey and chicken), and meat are from regions other than the one you live in. Chances are, you'll find a lot. You may find Kobe steaks from Japan, caviar (fish eggs) from Iceland, or salmon from Alaska. How is it possible that all of these meats and types of fish are available to us fresh and around the corner? Refrigeration, of course. Without the ability to keep our food cold it would spoil and go rotten before it ever got to the grocery store. The second a piece of fruit is picked or a slab of meat is cut, bacteria is trying to get into the food and spoil it. For the first 99 percent of human existence, electricity and refrigeration did not exist.

Food preservation is a major reason humans can live in so many different environments. If you live in a place with cold, snowy winters, there are probably only a few (if any) plants and vegetables that can grow year-round. Before meat and produce were so easily shipped (think sailboats and wagons) it was a community's ability to preserve what was reaped (picked) in harvest season that was able to sustain them throughout the harsh winter.

In this mission you take on the role of anthropologist to explore how humans preserved their food throughout history.

DRYING: Drying is the oldest and simplest food preservation system. It's exactly what you think it is: getting the food in a hot, dry environment so that the moisture leaves the food. Bacteria need moisture to thrive, so removing it makes it harder for the bacteria to multiply and spoil it. When people dry food they must be careful not to make the heat hot enough to cook the food, just warm enough to get the moisture out. Foods that people commonly dried were fruits, vegetables, fish, and meat. Sometimes, if the person lived in a hot enough environment, the food could be placed in the sun all day and that would be enough to dry it out. In colder climates, people would use fire to dry their food. This dried food could then be stored for months and eaten later. You've probably eaten a very common dried food yourself: raisins!

PICKLING: You have probably eaten a pickle before. Did you know that "pickles" are actually preserved cucumbers? When we pickle something we put it in vinegar (or another acid), and the acid prevents bacteria from getting to the food. All kinds of foods can be pickled. Kimchi (a staple in Korea) is pickled cabbage and radishes. In Great Britain people eat pickled onions and pickled eggs. Other foods like beef, fish, olives, and peppers can all be pickled. This was very handy for people living before refrigeration. You could take almost any food, put it in a jar with vinegar, put it in your cellar, and then eat it whenever you wanted.

SALTING: Another important food preservation technique was salting. As the name implies, this involves putting generous amounts of salt on a piece of meat. This draws out the moisture, and the salty environment makes the meat less likely to be invaded by bacteria. This was very important for sailors like Christopher Columbus and the navies of Old England. They would store huge drums or kegs of raw meat in a salty solution to keep it fresh for their long journeys around the world.

Now that you know a little about the history of food preservation, let's get hands on and try it ourselves.

Learning the Lingo

bacteria: Some of the smallest types of organisms on Earth. When fruits and vegetables are picked, or fish or animals are killed, bacteria that are all around us immediately try to invade and "eat" our food. Think of bacteria as nature's garbage men. They break down all the dead and decaying plants and animals; without them there would be quite a buildup! These bacteria are what cause food to go bad and spoil. Refrigeration, drying, pickling, and salting are all ways we, as humans, try to fight these bacteria and keep our food safe for us to eat.

drying: This is the drying out of food to preserve it. The goal is to get as much moisture out of the food, as moisture attracts bacteria that can spoil your food. Drying was traditionally done by fire or, in warmer climates, by the sun.

pickling: The food preservation technique in which food is put in vinegar (or another acidic solution), which stops the bacteria from attacking the food, therefore making it safe for humans to eat months, or even years, later.

salting: This food preservation technique involves putting salt all over raw meat. The salty environment inhibits (stops) the bacteria from collecting on the food and makes it safe to eat at a later date.

✴ ***Very Important!*** *Because this mission involves making hot items using the stove or microwave, you need to have a parent or responsible adult do this activity with you.*

Materials

- 4–8 mason jars
- 1½ lbs. clean Kirby cucumbers
- ½ cup apple cider vinegar
- 8 cups water
- ⅓ cup sea salt
- Optional ingredients (for flavoring): garlic cloves, dill seed, or dried red pepper

Plan of Attack

1.   First, make sure to either boil the mason jars and lids or clean them thoroughly.

2.   Take your clean cucumbers and put them in your jars, standing them up vertically. You can either leave them whole or cut them lengthwise into halves or quarters. If you cut them, the pickling process will go faster.

3.   Now here is where you can get creative. You can add garlic (1–2 cloves), dill seeds (1 teaspoon), or red pepper flakes (½–1 teaspoon) for flavor. Remember, we are trying to complement, not overpower, the taste of the pickles here.

4.   Next, mix the salt, apple cider vinegar, and water together in a pot and bring to a boil. This solution is called the *brine*. Brine is just a fancy term for a saltwater solution that people have used for centuries to tenderize food.

5.   Let the brine sit for about 5–10 minutes after boiling and then (very carefully) dump the brine into the jars. Try to fill as close to the top of the jar as possible.

6.   Put the tops on the jars as soon as they are full.

7.   Your pickles can be eaten in about three hours. Try one, and if you like the level of pickling, put the jar in the refrigerator. The cool temperature in the fridge will slow the pickling process. If you want it to pickle longer, simply leave the jar out.

8.   Once you do decide to put the jars in the refrigerator, the pickles will stay fresh for 2–3 weeks.

Take It to the Max!

Beef jerky, one of America's favorite snack foods, started as a way to preserve meat. Do some research on jerky. Find out why it was developed and how it is done, and then try to make your own.

THE SILENT BUILDUP: CHOLESTEROL, FATS, AND OIL

Content Area: Chemistry
Primary Skills Focus: Exploring Connections

Mission Objective: Absorb important facts about fats, oils, and cholesterol and what they can do to the human body. See firsthand the difference between healthy alternatives and fatty animal oils.

It seems like every time you watch TV, look on the Internet, or go to a restaurant, someone is talking about cholesterol and how your diet affects the health of your body. How can the food choices you make now have a big impact on how healthy your body and heart will be in the future?

The next time you hear about a certain food having too much cholesterol you will be able to understand the full story. In this mission you take on the role of nutritionist to learn about cholesterol, fats, and cooking oils. You may even become a master chef by learning how these fats and oils affect your cooking.

Learning the Lingo

artery: A blood vessel that carries blood from your heart to other parts of your body. You even have arteries that supply blood to the muscles that make your heart beat. These vessels that give blood to your heart muscles are called your *coronary arteries*.

cholesterol: A waxy substance used in your body to make many other substances, including hormones and Vitamin D. It is also used to protect the different cells and nerves in your body.

cooking oil: An edible liquid that is made up from fat that is obtained from plants. You may have eaten some of this cooking oil if you have ever dipped bread into olive oil. Olive oil is a type of cooking oil made from the liquid fat inside olives.

fat: In terms of your diet, a fat is a soft, greasy substance that is made up of something called *lipids*. You can find fats in vegetables and you can also find fat in meats. Have you ever noticed the grease on your pan after making a hamburger or bacon? This is the fat that has come out of the meat.

plaque: Fatty buildup on the walls of blood vessels in your heart that can lead to heart disease. This can be caused by an unhealthy diet, lack of exercise, or just genetic predisposition (your family history). Think of it this way: The blood vessels in your heart carry blood to nourish its muscles so it can pump correctly. If there are plaques building up in your blood vessels, not as much blood can travel through to your muscles. That leads to heart disease.

Materials

- 3 small containers, like yogurt cups or small bowls with covers, or 3 sturdy plastic food storage bags
- Olive oil
- Butter
- High fat ground beef (25% fat or higher) or regular bacon
- Pan or microwave-safe dish
- Microwave or stove

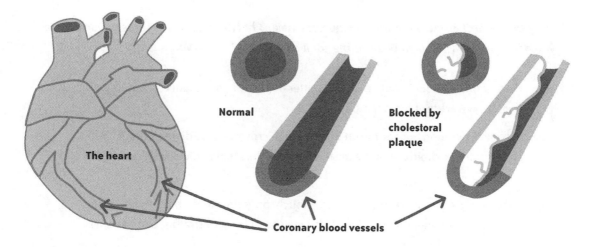

The heart

Normal

Blocked by cholestoral plaque

Coronary blood vessels

Plan of Attack

Where does cholesterol come from and why does our body need it? Cholesterol can be made inside your body from your liver, or you can get it from the foods you eat. Cholesterol is a type of lipid (fat) produced in the liver that is found in all animals (don't forget people are animals too!).

Cholesterol can be used in protecting different cells in your body, including your nerves and brain cells. Cholesterol helps us digest other fats, like the fat on the outside of a steak. We need cholesterol in our bodies, but too much cholesterol in your body can cause problems. Cholesterol travels through our blood inside our arteries and veins. When we have too much cholesterol in our bloodstream it can cause deposits of cholesterol plaques to stick to the walls of our blood vessels. The more plaques that are inside your blood vessels taking up space, the less blood can travel through those vessels.

The good news is that the amount of fat we eat, and the types of fat we eat, can affect how much cholesterol we have in our blood. Eating less fast food, fatty meats, and cheeses with high amounts of oils and saturated fats can lower your cholesterol. Remember, having high cholesterol gives you a higher chance of having plaques build on the walls of your blood vessels. Eating less fat decreases the cholesterol in your blood stream, and using unsaturated fats like olive oil and canola oil can also help do this.

But it can be tricky to tell what foods have high fat, high cholesterol, or both. One easy thing to remember is that vegetables might have fat in them, but only animal products have cholesterol. To make your diet a little bit healthier, try using plant fats for cooking instead of animal fats that have high cholesterol. Remember the cholesterol in animal fat can clog up your blood vessels by forming those plaques. It is like if you had bubble gum stuck inside your straw and then you tried to use that straw to drink something. Not much, if any, liquid would come through the straw. Plaque in your blood vessels keeps enough blood from flowing.

To really understand this concept, you are about to see the different forms of plant oils and animal oils and see if you can decide, by looking and feeling, which is the better choice for your body.

✳ ***Very Important!*** *Because this mission involves making hot items using the stove or microwave, you need to have a parent or responsible adult do this activity with you.*

1. Place a small amount of olive oil and butter in each of your small containers or bags. Leave aside at room temperature.

2. Place your ground beef or bacon in a pan or microwave-safe dish and cook until the fat starts to drain out of the meat. Wait until the meat and dish are cool to the touch.

3. When the grease and dish are cooled enough, pour the grease from the meat into your third container or ziplock bag. You may need to use a strainer to make sure the grease can be poured.

4. Leave the oil and fat for 30 minutes until the grease hardens and the butter is slightly melted.

Brain Buster Questions

1. Look at the different fats and oils. Which one looks like it would flow through a straw or blood vessel easier? Which one looks more solid?

2. Since all of the fat is cooled, dip your finger in each of the types of fat. What does each one feel like to you? Can you tell which one seems more solid?

3. Now try to wash your hand off in water without using soap. After you have rinsed your hand off, what do you notice about the fingers you dipped in the fat? Do they still feel greasy or sticky? (After this you can wash with soap and water until your fingers are no longer greasy.)

4. Which type of fat overall do you think may be healthier for your body?

You can now see that different fats have different forms. We know that we need fats in our body to protect us, but too much cholesterol can cause plaques inside your body that stick to your blood vessels. It is similar to that greasy/sticky feeling on your fingers after dipping them in the fat. You should be able to see how the fat from your beef or bacon became more solid and didn't look as clean as the olive oil. You can see how the more solid the fat, the harder it would be for it to move through something like a straw. Plant oils, like olive oil, are better for your body because they don't have the cholesterol that the fat from your beef or bacon does.

Now that you have seen how fat works outside your body you can understand how it affects the inside of your body and make smart choices to keep your body healthy.

Take It to the Max!

Have you noticed we talked about unsaturated fats? Have you heard of monounsaturated and poly-unsaturated fats? Find out how the molecular bonds of different fats affect our body.

THE ORIGINAL SOLAR PANEL: HOW LEAVES HARNESS ENERGY

Content Focus: Chemistry
Primary Skills Focus: Investigating and Classifying

Mission Objective: Become illuminated on photosynthesis and how plants take their energy from the sun. Use a tree key to identify the trees in your area.

You hear a lot about "green energy" these days; people are trying to get the energy they need without harming the environment. Did you know plants have been doing this for millions of years? They get all the *food* they need from something you see every day: the sun. Plants are able to convert the energy in the sun's rays to energy they need to grow using a chemical process called *photosynthesis*.

You've seen solar panels that people use to convert the sun's energy to electricity, but did you know that is the reason plants and trees have leaves? Leaves act as the solar panel of the plant: they take in the sun's rays and convert them to simple sugars to use for energy, the same way your body converts a peanut butter and jelly sandwich to give you energy. This is also the reason that most trees and plants are green; there is a molecule called *chlorophyll* in the leaves of plants and trees that can turn sunlight (and carbon dioxide) into food for the plant. The chlorophyll's green tint gives plants and trees their color. These natural solar panels come in different shapes and sizes, but they are all able to make energy. In this activity you will learn how to find out what kind of tree you are looking at just by examining a leaf.

Learning the Lingo

To identify your leaves (and trees) you will need to know a bit about the parts of the leaf. Here are some definitions that will help you.

alternate and opposite branching: This refers to how the leaves grow out from the stem. If the leaves on different sides of the stem match up, they are opposite. If not, they are alternate.

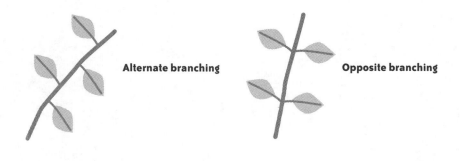

Alternate branching   Opposite branching

compound or simple leaf: A compound leaf has multiple "leaflets" coming out of one bud. A simple leaf has only one leaf coming out of the bud.

Simple leaf   Compound leaf

photosynthesis: The chemical process in which plants, trees, and other organisms convert sunlight, carbon dioxide, and water to energy using chlorophyll.

toothed leaf: A leaf edge that is toothed has a jagged edge, like a serrated knife.

Toothed leaf

Smooth leaf

Materials
- Tree key (page 46)
- Leaves from a few different trees

Plan of Attack

Go outside and, with permission, collect a leaf from several different types of trees. The tree key provided here will help you figure out what kinds of trees your leaves came from. Remember to look closely; small differences (toothed leaf, compound, etc.) can make a big difference in determining tree species.

Tree Key

Balsam Fir

Balsam Poplar

Basswood

Beech

Big-toothed Aspen

Black Cherry

Black Locust

Butternut

Eastern Cottonwood

Eastern Hemlock

Eastern Red Cedar

Elm species

Mountain Ash

Musclewood

Northern White Cedar

Paper Birch

Quaking Aspen

Red Maple

Red Oak

Red Pine

Shagbark Hickory

Sugar Maple

Tamarack

White Ash

White Oak

White Pine

White Spruce

Willow species

Yellow Birch

Take It to the Max!

Plants and trees aren't the only organisms that use photosynthesis for energy. Have you ever been to a pond and seen some murky, sludgy algae growing on the surface? What color is it? That's right, it's green because of photosynthesis. Find out how scientists are trying to use algae to make biofuel to power cars.

Leaf images after Sheri Amsel, exploringnature.org, used with permission. Identification information courtesy of LEAF, WIDNR Division of Forestry and UW–Stevens Point (leafprogram.org).

THE BRIGHT SIDE OF DECOMPOSITION: PLANTS, PRESSURE, AND OIL

Content Area: Chemistry
Primary Skills Focus: Measuring and Observing

Mission Objective: Unearth amazing facts about decomposition and how oil is formed. Create your own compost pile and see how nature can break down organic compounds.

You are about to dig up some secrets hidden underground for millions of years by learning about one of our natural resources—oil! If you look close enough you will see that oil, in its many different forms, is a resource we have on Earth that probably plays a big role in your everyday life even if haven't noticed it before.

You may not know that there are many different kinds of oil, and oil can come from many different sources. The oil we are talking about, crude oil, comes from miles below us underground and is used to form gasoline and motor oil. Some people are worried that someday we will run out of crude oil and we won't have enough to use in our everyday lives. How can we understand this problem?

In this mission you will take on the role of geologist and learn how crude oil is formed, where it comes from, and how it can be used. You will also get a chance to start the process of forming this natural resource with your own two hands.

Learning the Lingo

crude oil: A type of fossil fuel that is found deep underground and is processed to become petroleum, or gasoline.

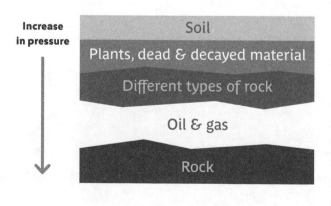

Increase in pressure

Soil

Plants, dead & decayed material

Different types of rock

Oil & gas

Rock

decompose: When natural materials are broken down physically and chemically into simpler forms. When an apple starts to turn brown and squishy after you leave it on the counter too long, it has started to decompose.

natural resources: Something that is found in nature and that is useful or necessary for humans in everyday life. These natural resources can be fresh water sources, forests and trees, minerals in the soil, and crude oil.

oil: A name for many substances that can be from minerals, vegetables, or even plant and animal fats. Oils are generally slippery, combustible, or have a liquid form. This includes oils that you can eat, like olive oil, and oil for your car, like motor oil.

pressure: An effect that occurs when force is applied to some surface. When someone shakes your hand and squeezes it lightly, this is an example of pressure being applied to your hand. Pressure can be applied to many things, and the soil and rock underground has pressure applied on it too.

Materials

- ½-gallon, cardboard milk carton
- Scissors
- Nails
- Small amount of soil
- Shredded newspaper
- Compost waste such as fruit peels, cut grass/yard waste, leaves, sawdust, vegetable peels, seeds, coffee grounds, or eggshells
- Duct tape

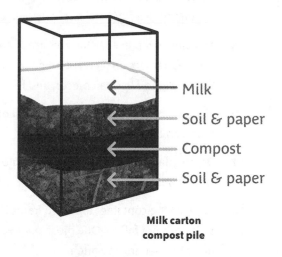

Milk

Soil & paper

Compost

Soil & paper

Milk carton compost pile

Plan of Attack

Crude oil is found deep underground, anywhere from a few hundred feet to a few miles. This crude oil, that we use to make gasoline, is removed from the ground by drilling deep into the earth.

How did this oil get down underground? Where did it come from? Well, crude oil was formed naturally on Earth over a long, long time. It took hundreds of thousands to millions of years to make this oil by a long process known as decomposition. Scientists believe that organic material, like dead plants and animals (including marine life), accumulated at the bottom of the sea, swamps, and rivers. Over a long time period the dead plants and animals get mixed with the surrounding soil and mud. As more and more of this dead organic material is formed it piles on top of the last layer. The deeper layers start to turn into rock and pressure starts to build up below the surface. Heat and pressure transform this organic material, over hundreds of thousands of years, to crude oil and gas. This is the same stuff we get out of the ground today.

Today we drill deep into the earth and get this oil and gas from underground to use in our daily activities. It can take millions of years for the crude oil to form underground, yet billions of people around the world use oil every day. The net result is that humans are using crude oil faster than nature can make it. That is why people are looking into different forms of energy for us to use, like wind and solar energy.

You are about to see firsthand how the process of decomposition breaks down organic matter, which is the beginning of fossil fuel formation. See for yourself how the process works by building something called a *compost pile*.

1. Take your milk carton and carefully cut off approximately the top one third. You should now be able to reach into the container to place things inside.

2. Keep the top of the container you have just cut off.

3. Carefully press a nail into the top and sides of the container. Make at least 10 to 12 holes on the top and 10 to 12 holes on the side portion of the top of your container.

4. Place a small amount of soil and finely cut newspaper shreds in the bottom of the container. Use a 2/3 soil to 1/3 newspaper mix to start.

5. You can now place a small amount of compost materials on top of the soil and newspaper mixture. It is recommended to start with a small amount of dead leaves, ripped in small pieces, and fruit peels cut in small pieces.

6. Place a small amount of dry, finely cut newspaper shreds over the top of this layer followed by a small amount of soil.

7. Do not place meat, dairy, or oil/fats into compost as they will decay and tend to smell bad.

8. Replace the container top (with holes in it) on the container. Tape the top in place so it does not fall off. One piece per each edge should be sufficient as you will need to open the top often.

9. Place the container in an area of the house that has stable temperature with some natural sunlight (windowsill, counter, etc.). You may want to choose an out-of-the-way area as these compost piles can smell.

10. Take the top off and mix compost daily. You can add more compost waste as you mix, and repeat step 6 each time.

11. It is important to keep your compost the right level of dryness to wetness. You want your compost somewhat damp, but not dripping wet. If the compost appears too dry, add a small amount of water, and if too wet add more finely cut newspaper to the mix.

You can start to see the contents decay over the first one to two weeks, but it may take up to four weeks to have fully useful new soil. Each time you mix your compost pile you can see how your materials are changing. In a few weeks you will see how organic materials decay and form soil. Now imagine having to wait a million years for crude oil to form underground!

Take It to the Max!

Natural resources can be grouped into renewable and nonrenewable resources. Find out what renewable and nonrenewable resources are and see where crude oil fits. Learn all about renewable energy.

ARE YOU A MOSQUITO MAGNET? TO LEARN AND PROTECT

Content Area: Chemistry
Primary Skills Focus: Exploring Connections

Mission Objective: Get the buzz on how mosquitoes sense their prey and spread disease. Then make your own mosquito repellent.

Have you ever heard somebody say, "Mosquitos really like me" because they seem to get bitten more than other people? In a way they might be right.

Mosquitos have special ways to find humans so they can bite them and get nourishment from their blood. You are about to learn ways mosquitos find you, what problems can come with mosquito bites, and how to protect yourself from them. You will even be able to make your own repellent and see if you can fend them off yourself.

Learning the Lingo

DEET: A chemical compound that is short for N,N Diethyl-meta-toluamide. It is used as insect repellent, helping to repel mosquitos and ticks. DEET is thought to work by having a smell that mosquitos really dislike, so they don't come near enough to bite you. Is DEET safe? There are different opinions, but it seems that lower concentrations of DEET are safer for humans than high concentrations.

malaria: Malaria is a vector-borne disease that is transmitted by mosquitos.

sensory cell: Receptor neuron on mosquito antennae that can sense skin odor or exhaled carbon dioxide. This can help them find their prey.

thermosensation: The ability to sense thermal (temperature) change. Warm-blooded animals give off heat and this heat can be a way for the mosquitos to find their prey.

vector-borne disease: A disease, or infection, that is transmitted to animals and humans by an insect. This is how certain infections are spread. A "vector" in this definition is just anything that transmits and carries a disease.

Materials

Repellent 1

- 1 cup dried rosemary leaves
- 4 cups water
- Medium-sized pot
- Strainer
- Large bowl or container
- Spray bottle

Repellent 2

- 2 cups white vinegar
- Fresh mint or catnip leaves (approximately 1½ cups)
- Bottle or jar with lid
- Strainer
- Large bowl or container
- 1 cup water
- Spray bottle

Plan of Attack

You may not have given a lot of thought to mosquitos, except for the fact that you probably find them annoying. Yes, mosquitos, female mosquitos to be exact, bite humans to get blood to help nourish them before they lay their eggs. Sometimes you get an annoying, itchy, red spot on your skin—a reaction that your body has to the irritating bite. But after it goes away you may not have thought much about it.

But did you know that mosquitos can transmit serious diseases between the different living creatures it bites? Malaria, a vector-borne disease transmitted by mosquitos, kills thousands of people a year, especially in places like Africa and Asia. People get sick with malaria when a mosquito bites an infected person and then bites someone else.

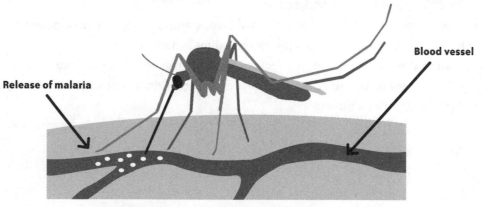

Release of malaria

Blood vessel

Mosquito bite releasing malaria parasite

How can we prevent these diseases? One way is to keep the mosquitos from biting you. Mosquitos have learned to find living things to bite by using chemical, visual, and heat sensors. Why is it important to know how mosquitos find the humans to bite? If we know how they find us, we can figure out how to hide ourselves or how to repel mosquitos.

Two ways mosquitos can find you are by the way you smell when you sweat and the heat your body gives off. One way to repel mosquitos is to use a repellent containing the chemical DEET. While some scientists claim that DEET is safe to use on the skin, others warn against use due to potential side effects. There are items in nature that also give off smells that mosquitos don't like and can make you less attractive to a hungry mosquito. By using these items you can trick the mosquito's chemical sensors and you may get bitten less. Now that you understand techniques that mosquitos use and why it is important to keep them from biting humans, you are halfway there. Take the next step by using some natural products to make your own mosquito repellent.

✳ ***Very Important!*** *Because this mission involves making hot items using the stove, you need to have a parent or responsible adult do this activity with you.*

REPELLENT #1

1. Pour water into your pot.

2. Place dried rosemary into the water, and bring to a boil.

3. Boil the water and rosemary for 5–7 minutes.

4. Let the mixture cool for 10–15 minutes.

5. When completely cooled, pour the mixture through a strainer into a bowl or container; discard the reserved rosemary.

6. The strained water should smell strongly of rosemary. Carefully pour the water into a spray bottle, and use this as your own mosquito repellent.

7. When the liquid stops smelling of rosemary, you can discard it and make more.

REPELLENT #2

1. Pour the white vinegar into a bottle or jar.

2. Crush or mash your catnip or mint in your hands and place it in the bottle or jar with the vinegar.

3. Put the lid on tightly and shake the mixture daily for at least three days (you can wait up to a week).

4. After you have waited at least three days, pour the mixture through a strainer into a bowl or container; discard the reserved catnip or mint.

5. Add 1 cup of water to the strained vinegar and stir. Carefully pour the water into the spray bottle and place in the fridge for use anytime.

You now have two homemade mosquito repellents. Rosemary and catnip are natural substances that, similar to the way DEET works, repel mosquitos because they don't like the smell.

Take It to the Max!

You have already learned that mosquitos have special senses to help them find a way to get their food. Did you know there are animals that have developed special ways to survive while living only in the waterfalls and rivers that go through very dark caves? Research how these animals live in such isolated and special places.

PART III

LANGUAGE ARTS

TAKE SHELTER, THERE'S A BRAINSTORM ROLLING IN! THE STARTING POINT OF CREATIVE WRITING

Content Area: Language Arts
Primary Skills Focus: Creative Expression

Mission Objective: Uncover some creative writing basics and then use this knowledge to "fill-in" a fun and engaging story.

Have you ever wondered how writers come up with those great ideas for all the books that you have read? Sometimes it seems that the stories have ordinary, uneventful beginnings, but the author fills the story with interesting twists and turns and makes it something very interesting to read.

In this mission you will become an author and learn about the art of creative writing as well as some techniques that can help you come up with great ideas for your own writing. After mastering these techniques you will challenge yourself by coming up with your next great story, with a little help of course!

Learning the Lingo

brainstorming: Traditionally, brainstorming has been a technique used in a group to help come up with a large number of ideas at one time. In creative writing, "individual brainstorming" can be done to come up with ideas to write about. There are specific techniques used in individual brainstorming, such as free writing, free speaking, and word association.

challenge: A demanding or stimulating situation. You might say, "I already knew that," but remembering to put your fictional character in a challenging situation is very important when coming up with a good story.

creative writing: Any writing that is not academic, journalistic, or professional writing. Some examples of creative writing are short stories, novels, and epics.

fictional character: Usually a person who is shown in a play, story, or movie who is made up, or imaginary. A fictional character could also be an animal, fairy, wizard, mythical creature, and so on.

resolution: The solution to the problem that has been going on. For example, the resolution in a murder mystery is finding out who did the crime at the end of the novel.

writer's block: A phrase that means an author is trying to write a story—to think up ideas and plot— but nothing is coming to mind so he or she isn't able to write anything.

Materials

- Paper and writing utensil

Plan of Attack

Take a minute to think about some of your favorite stories. How did the authors use the ideas and techniques described here to make those stories so enjoyable? In many great stories you will find characters in interesting situations (which are the challenges) who have to find a way to resolve them (the resolution). It may seem easy to come up with those two things and write a good story, but it isn't always that simple.

That is why some authors use the technique of brainstorming to come up with new ideas. There are many possible ways to engage in individual brainstorming but some of the best to help in creative writing are:

FREE WRITING: Write, on a sheet of paper, for a set period of time about anything that comes to mind. You can start with a certain topic or just write about anything in general. Don't focus on forming specific sentences or paying attention to grammar.

FREE SPEAKING: This is the same idea as free writing but involves speaking your ideas out loud instead of writing them down. You can have someone else help you by writing them down, or record yourself.

WORD ASSOCIATION: Start with one word or phrase that is related to some idea of your story or book. Write that down on your sheet of paper, and then as fast as you can, write the next word or phrase that comes to mind underneath it. Continue this for each new word or phrase until you have enough words to help you come up with ideas for your writing.

Not all of the ideas you come up with while brainstorming are going to be great or even good, but that is not the point of brainstorming. The point is to let your mind be turned on in a creative mode and to have many ideas to choose from, good and bad, that can provide inspiration in your stories.

Remember that stories become interesting when the character has a goal, confronts obstacles in reaching that goal, and finally resolves the challenges to reach the goal. For example, if a girl lost her dog and found the dog right outside the door, the story would be boring. What if the girl lost her dog, and the dog had jumped on the back of a truck going cross country, and now the girl had to find a way to follow the dog until she got it back? That would be a much better story! Now it is your turn. Test your skills by making your own interesting story.

You are about to read the beginning few sentences and the last few sentences of a story. It is up to you to come up with the middle! Remember, it's important to include things like challenge and resolution to make your story great.

Story Beginning

Jake wiped the sweat from his forehead as he shielded his eyes from the sun. Taking two deep breaths, he could feel his heart race as he tried to remember all the first-aid and survival tips he had learned last summer. The area of his brain that should have housed all of these tips—ways to start a fire, how to splint a broken arm, and ways to keep warm in a blizzard—was unfortunately completely empty. Cursing himself, he kicked the side of the large oak tree as hard as he could. Immediately regretting the move, he yelled out in pain and fell to the ground, staring up at the sky between the branches. Maybe it was the impact of the fall, or maybe just dumb luck, but as he stared up at the clouds he knew he had finally come up with a plan.

Story End

Walking up the driveway, Jake wanted to kiss the ground at his feet, he was so happy to be home. He knew, however, that this would look rather odd to anyone who may be watching.

"Mom, Mom!" he yelled, leaving the door wide open. "Where are you guys?"

From the backyard he heard his dog barking, and finally, he saw his father coming in through the screen door.

"Jake, you are back early! We didn't expect you home until tomorrow! How was your trip?"

Jake smiled and gave his dad a hug, wondering where to even start.

Now follow the instructions below to challenge your creative writing powers.

1. Brainstorm ideas by trying free writing, free speaking, and word association.

2. To help, you can brainstorm types of characters, then brainstorm a list of challenges, and finally come up with ideas for resolutions to these obstacles or challenges.

3. Next, using your idea list from the brainstorming, try to see how many different stories you can come up with using the same beginning of the story and same end.

4. Be creative! Use many different characters or just one. Use many different challenges or just one.

Take It to the Max!

Make a list of your favorite authors. Research and find out what, if any, writing techniques they use to write those books you love.

MARKING ITS WAY THROUGH HISTORY: THE STORY OF INK

Content Area: Language Arts
Primary Skills Focus: Exploring Connections

Mission Objective: Develop an understanding about the evolution of writing tools through history and then make your own ink using natural resources.

You are about to travel way back in time, to an era when cave dwellers were writing stories through artwork on the walls of their caves. Since that time, people have been writing down their stories to share with the world.

When you pick up a ballpoint pen and write, have you ever wondered what people did before it was invented? You are about to learn the history of how people throughout the ages wrote down their stories, how the pen and ink were developed, and even how you can make ink just like some of the pioneers of our country.

Learning the Lingo

ink: A pigmented liquid or paste especially used for writing or printing.

oak galls: Round, bulbous formations found on certain oak trees. These can be created by a reaction the tree has to being attacked by insects or other parasites. Inside of this mass there is a special spongy section and a seed. This part can be broken down and used to make special types of ink.

pigment: A substance used as coloring, which can be mixed with water, oil, or another product to make substances like ink or paint.

printing press: A machine used to press an inked surface to a cloth or paper.

William Shakespeare: Born in 1564 and died in 1616. He was a British author, famous for writing plays, sonnets, and poems. Many people consider him to be among the greatest writers of all time.

Materials

- ½ cup ripe berries (blackberries or raspberries work well)
- Fine strainer
- Glass mixing bowl
- Small jar or bottle with lid
- Spoon
- ½ teaspoon vinegar
- ½ teaspoon salt

Plan of Attack

Have you ever wondered how people wrote stories before they had computer printers, or even ball-point pens? We have come a long way from the time of cave dwellers scratching pictures on the walls of caves, and there have been many discoveries along the way.

Prehistoric humans used early inks made of sap, fruit pulps, and animal blood to tell their stories on rock walls. Later civilizations (such as the Sumerians that lived in the modern-day Middle East around 4000 BCE) codified a writing system, creating intricate stone tablets. In 2697 BCE a Chinese philosopher named Tien-Lcheu invented what we believe was the first ink. This ink was made to color the raised surface of stone carvings black. It was made by mixing the ashes of burnt pinewood with oil. At around the same time in history, almost halfway around the world in the country of Egypt, a kind of paper-like material was made from a plant called *papyrus*. The Egyptians were also developing an ink made from burnt oil and wood mixed with water.

In addition to many other contributions, the Ancient Romans (founded 753 BCE) made a pen-like device from marsh grass and bamboo. These plants had hollow centers that could be filled with ink, and the end would be cut to form a pen nib, which is just like the point of a pen.

When we think about old-fashioned writing, an image of the quill (feather-based pen) probably pops into our brains. This type of writing instrument was invented sometime between 600 and 700 CE in Seville, Spain. Quill pens were made from bird feathers that were sharpened to a point on the end. This point could be dipped in any kind of ink and be used for writing. At the time that William Shakespeare lived, many people used a special type of ink for writing called *Iron Gall ink*. Iron Gall ink is a purple-black ink made from the mineral iron, taken from the galls of certain trees, which was then mixed with acid. These ingredients were mixed together to give a strong colored, long-lasting ink.

Maybe the most important invention ever when it comes to writing books was the invention of the printing press by Johannes Gutenberg in the 1440s CE. This creation brought about the printing revolution and led the way for a faster and cheaper process for making books. Before this invention all books were handwritten, one by one. Now they were produced on the press and could be widely distributed. The first major book printed by Gutenberg was the Bible, which was made available to large amounts of people for the first time. Of course, even with the printing press, Johannes still needed ink to make his books!

You are now ready to make your own ink. People throughout history have used fruit-based ink, and you will learn their secret.

1. If your berries are not yet ripe, place them in the microwave for 15 to 20 seconds to soften them.

2. Place your berries in the strainer above the mixing bowl in the kitchen sink.

3. Smash the berries down toward the strainer using your spoon. A small amount of colored juice should come through the strainer into your bowl. Using your spoon, continue to smash then stir the berries against the strainer till only pulp and seeds

remain in the strainer and a thick juice sits in the bowl. The seeds and pulp from the strainer can now be discarded.

Mashing raspberries through strainer

4. Add the vinegar and salt to the "berry ink" in the bowl. This helps the ink keep its bright color and keeps it from spoiling.

5. If the berry ink is too thick, you can add small amounts of water to get the right consistency you need. Be careful not to add too much water or your ink will be hard to use and the color will be less bright.

6. Use your ink for stamping, or even try and make your own quill pen. (Hint: a wooden golf tee, chopstick, or BBQ skewer are other good alternatives. As always be careful with the sharp ends.)

7. You can save your ink by putting it in a covered jar or bottle and keeping it refrigerated.

You are on your way to becoming a master author and printer!

Take It to the Max!

After the invention of ink and paper many people used writing as a form of art, not just a way to communicate. Calligraphy is seen as one of these writing art forms. Find out what calligraphy is, and maybe even learn to write calligraphy.

WIZARD OF WORDS: METAPHORS AND SIMILES

Content Area: Language Arts
Primary Skills Focus: Creative Expression

Mission Objective: Explore the power of writing techniques such as alliteration, similes, and metaphors to understand how these methods can make writing so powerful. Using a short story, you will learn to recognize these techniques so you can employ them in your own writing.

You are about to become a wizard of the written word. Have you ever read something that has really made you picture exactly what the author is describing without having to think about it? It is almost like the writing is forming a movie that you see in your mind. Have you ever noticed that the writing of some authors is easy to read and with others you really have to concentrate on what they are trying to say? You are about to learn some tricks of the trade, some amazing techniques that could make you the next great author.

Learning the Lingo

alliteration: Repetition of a sound at the beginning of each word in a phrase. "Lucy's looking lovely!" is a phrase that uses alliteration. Do you see how the "l" sound is repeated in all three words? That is alliteration.

metaphor: Comparisons that show a common characteristic between two things that are not alike in most other ways. The phrase "her eyes are sparkling jewels" is a metaphor. The person's eyes aren't really jewels, but by using the metaphor you can tell the reader that her eyes are shiny.

onomatopoeia: A word that is able to imitate the sound it represents. Look at the word "zip." When you zip up your jacket, you also make the sound *zip*!

palindrome: A word, phrase, or number that can be read the same forward and backward. Look at the words "radar" or "level." Try spelling each word backward. It is the same word.

simile: A way to directly compare two things by using the words "like," "as," or "than." "Her eyes were as clear as the sky" is a simile.

Materials

- Paper and writing utensil
- Your powers of detection

Plan of Attack

Remember that book you read that made you feel like you were really there with the characters in their world? Have you ever been able to picture exactly what the characters were doing, clearly seeing what they looked like, where they lived, and how they acted?

This is no accident. The author has written the book with different techniques, or "tricks," to help you see and feel all of this while reading. There are many different techniques that writers use and you have just learned a few of these in the lingo section. By using some of these tricks in your own writing you can make your stories come alive too. The best way to learn and apply these techniques when you write is to first identify them in the writing of others.

Read the story here and watch for all of the things we have talked about. When you are finished, look at the questions that follow and see if you have become a wizard with words.

> *Is This a Dream?*
>
> *She didn't remember falling asleep, and as she stared silently at the world around her she also couldn't be sure if she was awake. There was a familiar feeling to the place but things looked slightly off. The blues of the sky were slightly brighter and the trees below were photocopies. Each one was evenly spaced with perfectly symmetrical branches. Much too perfect to be natural, she thought.*
>
> *She was awake, she concluded. "You can't smell in a dream," she told herself. And if she wasn't smelling the strong scent of the beautiful flowers, then why did the sneezing start? "Achoo! Achoo!" over and over, until she had convinced herself this could be no dream.*
>
> *If she wasn't at home, then where exactly was she? This is the question, she decided, that would be her focus. She looked at her watch. It was noon. She looked up to see the sun like a fire burning directly above her. The sunspots made her wince, but she managed to look again. This time there was no doubt. There were two moons like cat eyes looking down at her. She wasn't home. She was definitely not home.*

1. In the story see if you can find any metaphors, similes, alliteration, palindromes, or onomatopoeia.

2. Can you at least find five of these? (See page 64 for answers.)

3. Can you think of another type of writing that often makes use of alliteration?

4. Pick your favorite technique from above. Try to come up with three examples or sentences using these techniques.

5. Try to add the next paragraph to this story. Use at least one of these techniques in your next paragraph.

Take It to the Max!

One important aspect in telling a story is whose eyes the events are seen through. This is called the *point of view*. Learn what different points of view you can write from. Can you figure out what point of view your favorite book is written from?

Answers to #1 and #2:

- "she stared silently" alliteration
- "familiar feeling" alliteration
- "the trees below were photocopies" metaphor
- "smelling the strong scent" alliteration
- "Achoo! Achoo!" onomatopoeia
- "noon" palindrome
- "sun like a fire" simile
- "sunspots" alliteration
- "two moons like cat eyes" simile

THE SLEUTH OF TRUTH: A LITERARY TREASURE HUNT

Content Area: Language Arts
Primary Skills Focus: Investigating and Classifying

Mission Objective: Survey different types of literature such as poetry, prose, essays, and drama. You will then go on a "hunt" through your local library to find readily available classic works and determine which literary category they fit into.

You are about to uncover secrets about literature that have been hiding inside many of the most popular books in the world. Some of these books may even be on your bookshelf right now. With a simple trip to your local library you will learn about different types of literature, and with a little help, you will be able to uncover the hidden treasures of books that await.

Learning the Lingo

drama: A written story in either poetry or prose that is meant to be told by actors who are speaking the dialogue and acting out motions. Your school play is a form of drama.

fiction: A piece of literature not entirely true or factual.

nonfiction: A piece of literature based on fact. Examples include biographies, scientific studies, and historical essays.

poetry: A type of writing that uses the sounds and meanings of words in a specific structure to share thoughts and emotions. Many poems use certain patterns of rhyming or rhythm to produce artful expression.

prose: Prose can be thought of as "ordinary" writing. Prose doesn't have to follow a formal structure. One way to remember the difference is that prose is everything that is not poetry. In fact, you are reading prose right now.

Materials
- Access to your local library (and maybe some help from your friendly librarian)
- Paper and writing utensil

Plan of Attack

You have learned that literature can be broken down into poetry versus prose and fiction versus nonfiction, but how does that help you? Knowing about the different classifications of literature can give you insight on the author's motivation. Why did they write this book? Is it meant to inform? To entertain? To show how the author felt? You will now go on your own "literary treasure hunt" through the aisles of your local library.

1. Below is a list of some common books that are carried in most libraries.
    a. *The Call of the Wild* by Jack London
    b. *The Giving Tree* by Shel Silverstein
    c. *Hamlet* by William Shakespeare
    d. *Anne Frank: The Diary of a Young Girl* by Anne Frank
    e. *My People* by Langston Hughes
    f. *The Sign of the Beaver* by Elizabeth George Speare
    g. *The Adventures of Tom Sawyer* by Mark Twain

2. Try to find these books in the library. You may need the help of your librarian.

3. Don't be disappointed if you can't find all of these books. Your search will still help you learn about the exciting world of literature. Just find as many as you can at your library or home.

4. After you have found these books, look through them. Look at the way the words are written on the page, how the paragraphs are laid out, and even if they have (or don't have) chapters.

5. Now, try to read some part of the book. You don't have to read it all.

6. Can you make any guesses on what categories, prose or poetry, these books fit into?

7. If you decided the book is written in prose, which subcategory does it fit into? Essay, drama, nonfiction, or fiction? Remember, these categories can overlap, so you can make arguments that these books fall into more than one category.

8. Write an essay in the style of your favorite type of literature. Perhaps it is a piece of nonfiction prose on your favorite historical event. Maybe it's a poem exploring your feelings when something happened in your life. Be creative and have fun!

You now know some basics about literature and what a great variety of written works there are out there for you to explore. Use your newfound knowledge; who knows, maybe you will be the author of a book someday.

Take It to the Max!

The definition of poetry has been controversial to a lot of authors in the past and even to this day. See If you can come up with your own definition of poetry by investigating the many different types of poetry.

Answers to #6 and #7:

a. prose, fiction; b. poetry, fiction; c. prose and poetry, drama;

d. prose, nonfiction; e. poetry; f. prose, fiction; g. prose, fiction

안녕하세! WORLD WISE: LANGUAGES AROUND THE GLOBE

Content Area: Language Arts
Primary Skills Focus: Creative Expression

Mission Objective: Master how to say hello in many different languages and examine a map looking for patterns of language and speech across the world.

You are about to become a world traveler who can speak multiple languages right from your own house. Does anyone you know speak more than one language? Did you know that in some places in the world almost everyone speaks more than one language? Some people even make learning languages their career, and get paid to speak those different languages.

Languages aren't just cool to learn; knowing about different languages gives you a chance to learn about the people who speak those languages. Languages can be your key to unlocking some of the greatest treasures on earth.

Learning the Lingo

dialect: A form of a language that is spoken in a certain area or by a specific group of people. Did you know that we have dialects in the United States? In the state of Hawaii some people speak a dialect of English called *Pidgin English*. Don't worry, you would probably be able to understand most everything someone speaking Pidgin English would say, but it might just sound a bit different. For example, they might say, "Da water stay cold," which is the same thing as saying, "The water is cold." It's still English, just a different dialect.

language: A way to communicate thoughts and feelings using voice sounds and/or written symbols.

linguist: A person who has studied linguistics or somebody who knows how to speak several languages.

linguistics: The scientific study of languages.

translation: When talking about languages, translation is the act of re-telling something from one language into another language. A translator can help two people who speak different languages understand each other by translating for them.

Materials

- Map of the world (search online or check out a world atlas from the library)

Plan of Attack

Here is a table showing you how to say "hello" in different languages, along with the name of one country where each language is spoken. Pronunciation hints are given in parentheses. Practice saying each word out loud. You are becoming a linguist!

French	Bonjour (Bawn-ZHOOR)	France
Japanese	Kon'nichiwa (Ko-NEE-chee-wa)	Japan
Zulu	Sawubona (sah-woo-BOH-na)	South Africa
Turkish	Merhaba (mare-ha-bah)	Turkey
Hindi	Namaste (NAH-muh-stay)	India
Greek	Yassas (yah-sas)	Greece
Mandarin	Ni hao (NEE how)	China
Hawaiian	Aloha (a-LOW-ha)	United States
Gaelic	Dia Duit (dee-a ghwit)	Ireland
Xhosa	Molo (mo-lo)	South Africa
Spanish	Hola (OH-la)	Mexico

Brain Buster Questions

1. Can you read all the different ways to say "hello" in countries around the world?

2. Can you find all of these countries on a map of the world?

3. Do you see South Africa is listed twice on the list above? Can you think of a reason why they may speak more than one language in South Africa?

4. Spanish is spoken in many different countries around the world, from the country of Spain in Europe, to Chile all the way down in South America. Where did Spanish start? How did it get all the way from Spain to Chile?

5. Examine a world map (online or in an atlas) and determine if any of the countries on the map are near each other. Do their languages sound the same to you?

After reading all of your brain buster questions you might have even more questions about different languages. Languages are a way for people to share their thoughts and feelings; they can do this by speaking and/or writing the language. Just because countries are close together on a map doesn't mean their languages will sound similar. Even the same language, because of different dialects, can sound different when compared between people living in separate areas of that country.

We know that it is possible for one person to speak and understand many different languages, but don't forget, there are countries where different languages are spoken in different parts of the country. For example, South Africa has 11 official languages. On the eastern coast of South Africa, Zulu is the most common language spoken at home, but if you go farther west you are more likely to find people speaking Xhosa.

Examining the geography of language can lead to some interesting historical insights. The explorers to the areas that would become North and South America brought their own languages along with them, sharing these languages with new people at the same time. This helps to explain how the Spanish language was able to travel from its home in Europe to North and South America. You can now see why the study of languages is so interesting. Learning about languages makes it easier to learn about the people who speak those languages all over the world.

Take It to the Max!

In the United States you hear people speaking many languages, including English. One of the most popular languages spoken in the United States is Spanish. Is Spanish an official language of the United States? Find out if the United States has an official language.

HOW TO SIGN WHAT'S ON YOUR MIND: LEARNING SIGN LANGUAGE

Content Area: Language Arts
Primary Skills Focus: Creative Expression

Mission Objective: Investigate the history of Deaf communication throughout the world. Learn how to sign the alphabet, your name, and more.

Imagine what it would be like if you couldn't hear a person talking to you. What would you do? How would you communicate? Well, there are millions of people around the world who have figured out a way to communicate without needing to speak a word.

You may have seen someone at the grocery store or mall who was using the movement of his or her arms and body, along with making different shapes with his or her hands, to communicate with another person. This is sign language! There are many different types of sign language around the world, and sign language is the most common way the Deaf community uses to communicate.

You are about to step into a world where language isn't spoken or heard. In this mission you will learn about some of the history, and some of the prejudices, relating to the Deaf community. You will even learn some sign language yourself.

Learning the Lingo

American Sign Language: Also called *ASL* or *Ameslan*. This is the major language of Deaf people in the United States. ASL is also used in other countries, including Canada and Mexico. Just because people in a certain country speak English does not mean the people who use sign language in that country use ASL. The British speak English but have a different sign language.

"deaf and dumb": A phrase used in the past to refer to a person who was deaf and mute. The term "dumb" in this case refers to a person who is unwilling or unable to speak. This term is *not* accepted for use today, when the word dumb is usually used in place of the word stupid. We know that people who happen to be deaf or mute are clearly not less smart than anyone else, so the term "deaf and dumb" should *not* be used today.

deafness: Partial or complete loss of hearing. A person who is deaf either has no ability to hear or very little hearing that isn't useful for communication, in which case they may be called *hard of hearing*.

mute: Being unwilling or unable to speak. If you aren't speaking you may hear someone say, "What's wrong with you, did you go mute?" but the word mute can also refer to someone who is unable to speak for other different reasons. A person who is mute may also use sign language.

sign language: A language, just like spoken languages, that uses visually transmitted patterns instead

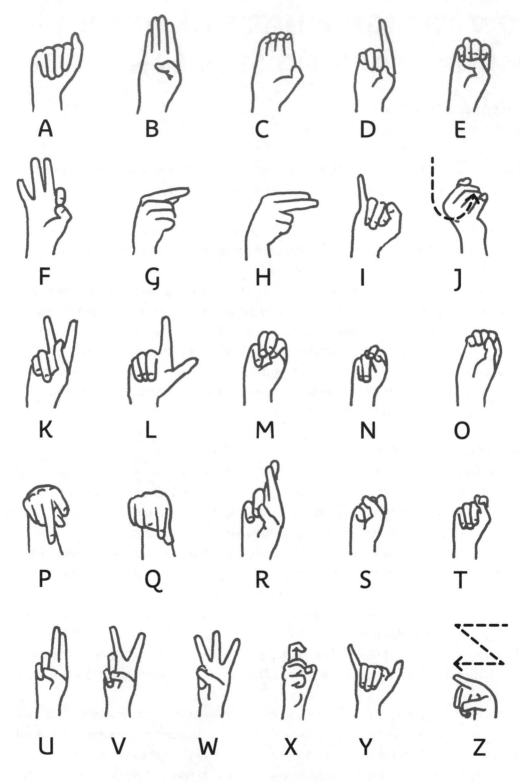

American Sign Language alphabet. Copyright 2008 StartASL.com

of acoustic, or "heard," sound patterns. What are these visual patterns? They can consist of many different parts, such as hand shapes, movement of arms and body, and/or facial expressions. Just like when you are speaking, people using sign language can use combinations of elements like facial expressions and movements of their body to help in understanding.

Materials

- Mirror
- American Sign Language alphabet chart (see page 72)

Plan of Attack

Although it may be hard to imagine, it was not that long ago that Deaf people in the United States were oppressed and denied equal rights. The ancient philosopher Aristotle believed that the only way a person could be educated was through the spoken word, meaning that Deaf people could not learn. Throughout the years, people who are deaf or mute have had to deal with being seen as unable to learn or be educated and have been denied rights that other people have had because of this prejudice.

Did you know that there was a time in the United States that Deaf people could not marry? Could not own property? And some were forced to have guardians. The laws have even gone as far as calling them "non-persons."

Slowly things started to change, and in Europe during the 1500s the Deaf began to be educated using writing. In 1771, the first public school for Deaf children was opened in France by Charles Michel de L'Epee. De L'Epee saw that some of his students were using "signs" to communicate, and through learning the signs he made the first standardized sign language. This sign language was called Old French Sign Language and was used in many parts of Europe.

An American, Dr. Thomas Gallaudet, used his teachings from schools in Paris and London to start the first free public school for the Deaf in the United Sates. It was at this school that American Sign Language was born. Over the years, sign language has become an accepted form for education and communication, and the Deaf have gained equal rights in the United States. Even so, it is important to remember the struggles to overcome prejudice and ignorance that the Deaf community has faced.

Now that you learned a little about sign language and the Deaf community, it is your turn to learn some sign language.

1. Sit in a position so you can clearly see yourself (and specifically your hands) in the mirror.

2. Try each letter of the ASL alphabet from A through Z.

3. Once you feel comfortable with the hand positions for all the letters, remove the ASL alphabet picture from your view and have a friend hold it.

4. Have them quiz you by asking you to make all the different letters and checking if you did them right on the chart.

5. You are now ready to use your ASL alphabet.

Many places have classes and groups that meet to teach and practice their sign language. If you really loved learning the alphabet, try to get in touch with these groups so you can learn to communicate fully with ASL.

Take It to the Max!

ASL may have seemed like a unique language to you, but there are many languages around the world that have unique properties. Did you know that there are "click" sounds as a major part of one of the languages of the world? You may have even learned about one in the last mission. Research languages that use something called *click consonants*.

PART IV

EARTH SCIENCE

DON'T MOVE—YOU'RE IN QUICKSAND!

Content Focus: Earth Science
Primary Skills Focus: Measuring and Observing

Mission Objective: Muck through the science behind quicksand and then make your own to demonstrate how it is formed.

We've all seen the movies. An adventurer turns a corner and is sucked into the earth by a pit of quicksand. When it seems the victim will be completely swallowed up, he or she is saved by grabbing a tree branch to hang on to and escape certain death! Is this for real? While quicksand does exist and has trapped people and animals in the past, it isn't as dangerous as the movies make it out to be. In this activity you will become an expert in quicksand—what it is and what to do if you are ever caught in it. You will even get to make your own.

Quicksand is formed when sand and water are mixed together in just the right combination. Normally, sand can support some weight. When too much water is mixed with sand, the sand particles become separated from one another by water. This is called *saturation*. Because of this, there is no friction in between the sand particles and they can't support any weight. What looks like a solid can quickly turn to a jelly-like liquid if you take a wrong step! You can see this principle when you visit a lake or beach. The driest sand is able to support you just fine, but you begin to sink more and more as you walk on more saturated sand.

Quicksand can be found anywhere water meets sand: beaches, marshes, lakes, or riverbanks. The formation of quicksand depends on factors such as how much water is in the sand, if there is motion to the water (standing water versus moving water), and whether a force (like an animal stepping in the sand) has disturbed the amount of pressure (or stress) on the sand. While it is common in the movies for heroes or villains to fall into quicksand and become stuck, in reality this is very rare. Most quicksand has a higher density (relative heaviness) than the density of the human body, so a human is not likely to completely sink in quicksand. However, it is true that the more you struggle, the harder it is to get out. The reason for this is that after the quicksand becomes a liquid, its viscosity increases, or thickens. This happens because as you flail around trying to escape, you are mixing up the water and sand, forming a thicker mixture called *sand sediment*. At first you can

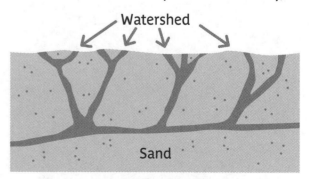

How quicksand is made

float on the quicksand but as you move around the sand and water particles becomes heavier (like concrete). Since you are now inside the heavy quicksand you find it hard to move. The harder you struggle, the harder it is to escape.

If you could add enough water to this thickened quicksand it would start to feel like you were floating again and it would be easier to move around. Experts say that if you get stuck, you should slowly spread your arms and legs apart and lean back. You should then float to the top. With that said, most quicksand pits are only a couple of feet deep and the human body is less dense than quicksand, so even if you do nothing, you should still float.

Learning the Lingo

density: The amount of material there is within the space that it takes up. For example, one cubic foot of brick is denser than one cubic foot of marshmallows. Quicksand is denser than the human body, so we will float in quicksand.

friction: The resistance encountered when one material moves past another. In our example, the friction of sand moving against itself is high, and can therefore support the weight of a person. But the friction of sand moving against water is low and we therefore initially sink.

saturation: A process that happens when no more of a substance (like water) can be absorbed or mixed with a different substance (like sand). When sand is saturated with water it becomes less dense and it can't support the same amount of weight that it can while dry.

viscosity: This is the measure of how thick the consistency is of a liquid. For example, water has low viscosity while maple syrup has a high viscosity. As people struggle in quicksand, they are increasing the viscosity and therefore making their escape more difficult.

Materials

- 2 cups cornstarch
- Mixing bowl
- 1–2 cups water
- Wooden spoon
- Small toy figure such as a person or animal

Plan of Attack

1. Pour the cornstarch into a bowl. Then, stir in one cup of water. It should look fairly chalky and pasty at this point. Mix in ¼ cup of water at a time until your mixture is not quite a liquid, not quite a solid. You don't want it too chalky, but you also don't want it too watery. You've just made quicksand!

2. This combination of cornstarch to water should saturate the cornstarch enough so it has all of the properties of quicksand. Test this by stirring the mixture together very fast. It should become denser and harder to stir the faster you go. If it's too

thin and soupy, you may have to add more cornstarch.

3. Quicksand interests people because it's almost halfway between a liquid and solid. When you are stirring or poking the mixture quickly, the corn flour grains are rubbing against each other as water is being pushed out with movement, making the mixture seem more like a solid. When you stir slowly the water stays between the grains and the whole mixture seems to liquefy.

4. Try to submerge a toy figure into the quicksand. Have the figure struggle to get out by thrashing it around. Compare that to slowly lifting it out. Different, right?

✳ *Note: Do not put quicksand down the drain; it may clog your pipes. Instead, put it in a plastic bag and throw it out with the trash.*

Take It to the Max!

You now understand that it is very unlikely for a human being to drown in quicksand. So why is quicksand still considered dangerous? Think about what other things could happen to you if you were stuck in quicksand for hours or days.

GETTING THE DIRT ON SOIL POLLUTION

Content Focus: Earth Science
Primary Skills Focus: Exploring Connections

Mission Objective: Explore different ways that humans pollute the soil beneath us. Complete an experiment in which you add different pollutants to plant samples and track their growth.

Next time you are walking around your neighborhood, look at the drains along the curbs. You may see a big sign posting **no dumping, drains to river** and a picture of a fish. Why do you think this is there? As you can probably figure out, these signs are there to remind us that everything we put down a drain or in a gutter will eventually end up back in nature. Many of the chemicals that we use every day can be very bad for the environment.

This wasn't always the case. Many scientists believe that humans have been around for 200,000 years and, for most of that time, we didn't have the technology or expertise to make chemicals like gasoline, household cleaners, or even plastics. It has only been in the last 150 years that most of these everyday chemicals have come into existence. While these chemicals have been great because they give us easy ways to clean our bathrooms, take paint off our walls, or keep insects off our crops, some of these products can really hurt the environment. In this mission you will assume the role of environmental scientist and focus on one part of the environment that can get hurt from pollution: the soil.

There are many different types of soil pollution. One of these is called *salinization*. Salinization is when there is too much salt in the soil, and plants have a hard time growing in those conditions. There are two main ways that soil can become salinized. One is the use of too much potassium fertilizer. Fertilizers are substances made to help plants grow. Too much of a potassium fertilizer will leave behind huge salt deposits that will hurt plant growth. Another cause for salinization is over-irrigation. All water (even rain water) has some salt in it. When plants are watered they use the water but the tiny bits of salt are left behind in the soil. Over time, these tiny bits of leftover salt can hurt plant growth.

Sometimes accidents pollute the soil and water. For example, in 1989 an oil tanker in Alaska, the *Exxon Valdez*, collided with a reef and spilled between 200,000 and 300,000 barrels of oil into the ocean. This was a disaster for the plants and animals along the coastline of Prince William Sound, where this happened. In 2010, a BP oil drilling rig called Deepwater Horizon exploded and the resulting oil leak, from a well on the ocean floor, could not be stopped for over two months. After the leak was capped, it was estimated that the oil well spilled about 4.9 million barrels of oil into the Gulf of Mexico.

Another way that humans pollute the soil is with the use of pesticides and insecticides. These are chemicals that are sprayed on crops and keep insects and other organisms away from farmers' crops.

The problem is that many of these chemicals are bad for a lot of organisms, not just the ones that eat the crops. When they get into the soil they can kill some of the smaller organisms like fungi or bacteria. These smaller organisms help plants grow and are good for the environment.

Learning the Lingo

control subject: A subject in an experiment where no factors are applied and no experimentation is performed. This is the subject against which the other subjects are compared.

pesticide: Chemicals sprayed on crops to keep insects and other organisms from eating them. Some of these chemicals can seep into the ground and kill organisms that are actually good for plant growth.

pollutant: A substance that is put into the air, water, or land that hurts the environment.

salinization: The process in which an area becomes too salty. This can happen from over-irrigating or the use of potassium fertilizer.

Materials

- 4 rosemary plants in 4-inch pots
- 1 cup water
- ⅓ cup salt
- ⅔ cup motor oil
- Shallow dish or pan

Plan of Attack

In this experiment you can see firsthand what can happen to plants (and maybe our food crops) if too many pollutants are put into the Earth.

1. Go with your parents or guardian to a local nursery, home improvement, or even grocery store. Try to buy four pre-potted rosemary plants. They will probably be growing in 4-inch plastic containers. Another option would be to buy seeds and grow the plants in your own containers following the directions on the package. Try to keep everything the same between the plants.

2. Now for the fun part. You are going to pour different additives into the soil to see how plant health can be influenced by what is in the soil. Plant #1 is your control. That means you don't do anything to it. As long as you follow the instructions for how to grow this plant, you can consider whatever this plant does as "normal growth."

3. Plant #2 will be the one you will try to oversalinize. Mix the water and salt. Stir vigorously and dissolve as much of the salt into the water as possible. Slowly pour the salt solution into the rosemary and soil in Plant #2. Any leftover salt in your

mixing cup can be scraped onto the top of the soil. This plant will replicate what happens when an area becomes salinized due to either over-irrigation or the use of certain fertilizers.

4. Pour the motor oil into the soil of Plant #3. You will need an adult to help you with this. Make sure there is a dish or pan beneath this plant as motor oil will most likely drip out of the bottom of the pot over the next day or so. This plant represents what can happen to plants when an oil tanker crashes or oil wells are uncapped, and thousands of barrels of oil are sent into the sea and along shorelines.

5. What goes into plant #4 is up to you. Try to think about something you have in your house that people sometimes pollute (either on purpose or on accident) into the environment. Some ideas of possible pollutants include window cleaner, laundry detergent, or paint (again, be sure you have adult supervision).

6. Now hypothesize (make your best educated guess) as to which plant will grow the largest or stay the healthiest. Which will show the effects of pollution first? Why do you think that? Write your hypotheses down on a piece of paper.

7. Try to have all of the plants in the same spot (so they get the exact same amount of sunshine). Give them the exact same amount of water. Observe their growth. Which plant grew the most? Which plant grew the least? Was it what you were expecting?

Take It to the Max!

You have explored some types of soil pollutants that can hurt plants' growth, but what can go into soil that can *help* plant growth? Repeat part of the experiment with different types of fertilizers (either from the store or homemade) in the soil instead of pollutants. See how this affects plant growth.

MORE THAN JUST A PRETTY TASTE: CRYSTALS

Content Area: Earth Science
Primary Skills Focus: Measuring and Observing

Mission Objective: Treat yourself to the chemistry of crystals and make your own sugar crystals to see these principles before your eyes.

Have you ever looked at a gemstone, like a ruby or diamond, and wondered how such a beautiful thing was formed? Have you ever sprinkled salt on your food and seen it disappear before your eyes, or caught a snowflake and wondered what it would look like under a microscope? Even though you may not realize it, all of these things have something very interesting in common—they are all crystals.

You are about to experience the wonderful world of crystals by learning about what they are and how they form. You will learn how to make your own crystals, and you can eat them, too!

Learning the Lingo

crystals: A solid substance, formed by a regular three-dimensional repeating pattern of molecules and atoms. This unique pattern isn't something you can necessarily see just by looking at the crystal. But if you could see down to the level of the atoms and molecules inside, you would see a pattern that keeps repeating in order to give the crystal its shape.

dissolving: Dissolving is a term used when two substances are combined, a solute and a solvent, to make a solution.

saturated solution: A solution that has the maximum amount of the solute dissolved inside it. In a saturated solution if you added any more solute it would no longer dissolve.

solute: In chemistry, a solute is the part of a solution that was dissolved when mixed with another substance (usually the liquid). Remember a solute mixed in a solvent is called a *solution*. To make a solution the two items have to mix together so they don't just become separate again. Sugar syrup is a solution, but pebbles in water are not.

solvent: A liquid that can dissolve another substance so that it becomes a part of the original liquid. This total mixture is called a solution. It is important to understand that the solvent doesn't change its "state." This is a fancy way of saying that this is not necessarily a permanent change to the original liquid.

Materials

- Pieces of cooking twine or cotton twine, or blunt wooden skewers/chopsticks (these items should be approximately the same length in height as the glass jar or tall glass used below)
- 2–3 cups sugar
- 1 cup water
- Pot
- Wooden spoon
- ½ teaspoon vanilla extract (optional)
- 1 glass jar or tall glass
- Clothespin
- Paperclip

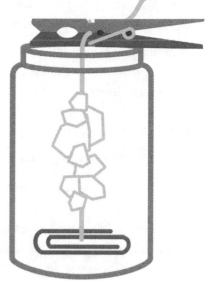

Setup to form sugar crystal candy

Plan of Attack

✳ ***Very Important!*** *Because this mission involves making hot items using the stove, you need to have a parent or responsible adult do this activity with you.*

1. Wash your twine or wooden skewer and gently roll it in a small amount of sugar so the surface is lightly covered. Let this dry completely before proceeding to step 2.

2. Place water in the pot on the stove and heat until the water starts to boil. When the water boils, begin to slowly add your sugar, stirring to dissolve, or mix, as much sugar in the water as possible.

3. Continue stirring the mixture until the sugar stops dissolving in the water. Stop adding sugar when it starts to collect in the bottom of the pot. The mixture should be clear but slightly thick. Turn the heat off while you continue to stir the mixture.

4. If you want your crystals to have a slightly vanilla taste, stir vanilla extract into the solution.

5. Let the solution sit until it is cool enough to pour into the glass jar (about 5 to 7 minutes). Pour solution into jar.

6. Attach one end of the string or skewer to a clothespin and lower the other end into the jar. Lay the clothespin across the opening of the jar so that the string or skewer stays in the middle of the jar or tall glass. Make sure it sits within the solution and doesn't float on the top (clip a paperclip to the end as a weight if needed).

7. With your string or skewer in place, let the mixture sit for approximately seven days or until much of the water evaporates.

8. Remove the string or skewer and you should have crystals attached to it. You have now made crystals! It is OK to eat these crystals because they are made out of sugar. Enjoy!

Brain Buster Questions

1. Can you name your solvent in this experiment?

2. Can you name your solute?

Even if you didn't know it, when making your homemade crystals, you were mastering how to use solvents and solutes and how to make a saturated solution. In this way of making crystals, the water is your solvent because you are mixing the sugar into it to be dissolved. This makes the sugar your solute, and together they make a solution. This solution has the maximum amount of dissolved solute, so you just made a saturated solution.

In your experiment one of the reasons why the dissolved sugar mixture ends up forming into larger sugar crystals is that the mixture cools slowly over time. In nature, some types of crystals form by a similar process of cooling liquid. One way that emeralds form is from liquid rock (magma) deep in the earth that starts to move up towards the surface of the earth. If this magma has the correct chemical makeup, as it moves toward the surface it cools and releases water, which can form emerald crystals.

Another process that happens to make your sugar crystal candy is evaporation. Evaporation is when a liquid substance turns into its gas form (vapor). Quartz crystals form in nature using this same principle of evaporation. When water that is filled with minerals starts to evaporate, the minerals left behind can form together in a repeating pattern, making quartz crystals.

Through making your own rock candy crystals and learning about solutes, solvents, and evaporation, you can now start to understand the complex world of crystals.

Take It to the Max!

We know that gemstones like rubies and diamonds are crystals, but did you know that diamonds are one of the hardest materials on earth? Find out all of the things diamonds can be used for besides jewelry.

AAHH. . . THE AIR WE BREATHE

Content Area: Earth Science
Primary Skills Focus: Investigating and Classifying

Mission Objective: Learn about air quality issues and the increase in air pollution in the industrial age. Then, take on the role of an EPA scientist and measure the air quality in different locations in your area.

Did you know that in some places the air itself can be "dirty"? That's right; many things that we do as humans contribute to our air quality. Over the past 150 years air quality has gotten significantly worse due to the ways humans have an impact on the environment. Many of these air quality problems have to do with the production of everyday goods. Even the production of the paper on which this is printed has contributed to air pollution. Just like roadside pollution that dirties a highway, factories can dirty the air by expelling dangerous gases that are produced in the creation of everyday items like clothes and electronics. If people are exposed to too many of these pollutants, they can develop health problems. These problems can be small, like a sore throat or irritated eyes, or they can be very serious, like asthma and heart disease.

Most of the time these pollutants are pushed out of the factories through smokestacks. Smokestacks are like big factory chimneys that take the leftover heat and gases that come from melting plastics or forging metals and put them out into the atmosphere. I'm sure you've seen these smokestacks when driving past a factory. Most states and cities have regulations (laws) about how much pollution can be released by factories into the air or water. This regulation of pollution is done through the government agency the Environmental Protection Agency (EPA). Even with these laws in place, you can still see the effects of pollution in many US cities. In big cities like Los Angeles and Houston you can see brown clouds of smog (a term combining smoke and fog) that hang over the city as a result of vehicle and factory emissions. In this mission you are going to take on the role of an EPA investigator and figure out the air quality of your city.

Learning the Lingo

air pollution: Very small pieces of debris or chemicals that hang in our air. Most of the time air pollution is caused by factories or vehicles.

emissions: The release, or discharge, of gases or chemicals into the environment by factories or vehicles.

Environmental Protection Agency (EPA): The US government organization dedicated to making sure the environment is safe for humans and other organisms.

smog: The word is a combination of smoke and fog. It refers to the foggy atmosphere produced by too much vehicle or factory emissions.

smokestack: A chimney structure (usually attached to a factory) responsible for discharging chemicals, gases, or heat into the environment.

Materials

- 4–5 white index cards
- Hole punch
- Marker
- Petroleum jelly
- String
- Magnifying glass

Plan of Attack

1. As an EPA agent, you have been assigned to find out what part of your town has the cleanest air. Choose 4 to 5 different places around your town or city from which to measure the air quality. Be creative; maybe choose a spot by a busy highway, another in a secluded park, etc. Try to pick spots that are out of the way so nobody will disturb your experiment. Hypothesize (make your best educated guess) as to which area will have the best air quality. Which will have the worst? Why do you think that?

2. Hole-punch the corner of each card. Label each card on the lined side with the location where you plan on hanging it.

3. Accompanied by an adult, take a card to each location and smear the unlined side with a thin layer of petroleum jelly. Try to do this when pleasant weather is expected, as snow or rain will ruin your results.

4. Loop some string through the hole in the card and hang it somewhere at each location where the jellied side will not touch anything—perhaps on a fence post or tree branch. Leave the cards hung up for about a week and then take each card down and bring it home. Be careful not to touch or disturb the jellied side of the card.

5. Take your magnifying glass and examine each card for air pollution particles. If you look closely you may actually see the pollution stuck to the cards.

6. What did you find? Did one section of town have worse air pollution when compared to another? Why? Do you think it would be different depending on the seasons? Is there a relationship between cars, factories, and the pollutants? Remember, you are the EPA government worker here and it is up to you to decide what part of town has the best air quality.

Take It to the Max!

Now you know that the United States has specific laws and regulations about how much factories can pollute our air, but what about other countries? Do some research about international cities and look at what happens when countries have loose rules about pollution. Study these cities and more:

1. Mexico City, Mexico   2. Sukinda, India   3. La Oroya, Peru
4. Dzerzhisk, Russia   5. Beijing, China

NOTHING NEW UNDER THE SUN: THE BEAUTY OF THE WATER CYCLE

Content Focus: Earth Science
Primary Skills Focus: Measuring and Observing

Mission Objective: Drink in some information about the water cycle and then construct a model simulating our atmosphere and cloud formation.

Go to the kitchen and get a glass of water. Do you have it? Now, take a guess as to how old you think that water is. Weird question, right? While that water just came out of your faucet a minute ago, the water is as old as the Earth itself. Your glass of water may have been, at one time, a refreshing drink for a Tyrannosaurus rex. It could have been used to clean the hull of the *Titanic* before its doomed voyage, or frozen in the iceberg that sank it! The point is that there is no new water ever created on Earth; it is recycled over and over again for billions of years.

You might ask how it can stay fresh. The answer is in the water cycle. There are four main stages of the water cycle: evaporation, condensation, precipitation, and collection. Evaporation occurs when the sun heats up bodies of water and turns the water molecules into steam or vapor. Only the fresh, clean water molecules are evaporated; the rest of the "junk" that can get in water is left on Earth. This is how the Earth purifies its water.

The invisible water vapor is in the air all around us, but from the ground it is usually invisible to us. As these water molecules rise in the sky they hit cooler air higher in the atmosphere. The cooled water vapor mixes with tiny pieces of dust, forming droplets that condense together to form clouds. When so much water has condensed together (or the temperature drops, forming small pieces of ice) these droplets in the cloud get larger and start to fall, forming precipitation. Precipitation can fall back to the Earth in the form of rain, hail, sleet, or snow. When the precipitation hits the Earth it either soaks into the soil or collects to form our rivers, lakes, and oceans.

In this mission you will see firsthand how this process works.

Learning the Lingo

condensation: The change from a gaseous state to a liquid state. One example of this is vapor from a lake condensing to form a cloud.

evaporation: The vaporization of a liquid. When liquids change from a liquid state to a gaseous (or vapor) state.

precipitation: Forms of water (rain, hail, sleet, or snow) that fall from clouds to the Earth. This happens when so much water has condensed in a cloud that the water droplets become so heavy they fall to the ground.

water cycle: The continuous movement of water on Earth. The way water is collected, purified, and distributed to living things and the environment.

Materials

- Small pot
- 4 ounces water
- Standard-sized (16 oz.) Mason jar
- Matches
- 1-gallon ziplock bag full of ice

Cloud formation

Plan of Attack

✳ **Very Important!** *Because this mission involves matches and boiling water, you need to have a parent or responsible adult do this activity with you.*

1. Bring the water to a boil in the pot, then carefully fill the jar with the water. Let it sit for a few minutes. It is important to fill the jar with hot water first to heat the sides. This will prevent too much condensation from forming during the experiment.

2. Pour out some water until the jar is about ¼ full.

3. Have an adult light a match, blow it out, and quickly toss it in the water. Immediately cover the top of the jar with a bag of ice.

4. You should see a cloud start to form inside the jar. Why does it do this? How does the temperature change that resulted by adding the ice affect the water?

This experiment showed you how clouds form. The water molecules on ground level become very warm, evaporate, and rise up. If you have ever gone to the top of a mountain, you know that the higher you go, the colder it gets. As the air gets cooler the water molecules come together and become clouds. This process is called *condensation*.

Take It to the Max!

Make a weather journal that focuses on clouds. A few times a day, go outside and make a note of the types of clouds above, the temperature, and wind conditions. After writing down these observations for a few days look for patterns and trends. Does it usually rain or snow at a certain time of day? Do certain types of clouds mean rain and snow while others indicate a pleasant day? Do some research on cloud types on the Internet or at your local library and try to classify the clouds in the sky. You may be on your way to becoming a meteorologist.

HEY FELLOW, WHY'S THAT PULP YELLOW? THE SCIENCE OF ANTIQUE PAPER

Content Area: Earth Science
Primary Skills Focus: Exploring Connections

Mission Objective: Analyze the chemistry and production of paper throughout history. Then, make your own paper from household goods.

Imagine that you have found a treasure chest buried years ago. When you open this chest there is a map inside. What do you think this map would look like? You probably picture an old, brittle, yellowish-brown piece of paper.

Over time most ordinary paper does turn brown or yellow. But why and how? To understand what happens to make those treasure maps look the way they do, you first have to understand how paper is made and the changes it goes through. You will also have the chance to make some old-time paper for yourself.

Learning the Lingo

absorption of light: When light rays hit an object the light will either be reflected (the light bounces back off the object) or absorbed (the light is taken in by the object). When some objects come in contact with specific wavelengths of light they can keep or absorb some of this light energy. Sometimes you can tell that light is being absorbed by a change in color that happens to the object being hit by the light. This is important in understanding why old paper looks the way it does.

cellulose: An organic, or natural, substance that is made up of carbon, oxygen, and hydrogen atoms. All living things are made up of cells, which are like building blocks. Cellulose forms the main part of the cell walls in plants. Cellulose is important in the cell walls of trees. So naturally, cellulose becomes the main part of wood.

lignin: Another substance found in the cell walls of trees that helps in making wood stronger and keeping it together.

wavelength: Even though we can't see it, light, like the light from the sun, is transferred in a form that looks like a wave. This wave has peaks and valleys just like a wave of water. The wavelength is the distance between one peak and the next peak, or one valley and the next valley. Why is this important? The characteristics of different wavelengths will affect how light is absorbed, and even what color things are. Do you know the reason the clothes you are wearing have different colors is partly because of the properties of wavelength?

wood pulp: A material made from separating wood. Pulp can be made in a few different ways. The most popular processes are mechanical (by machines) and thermal (by heat). Pulp is necessary to make paper.

Materials
- 2 pads fine steel wool
- 16 ounces distilled white vinegar
- Sealable disposable container (old water bottle, glass jar, rubber food storage tub, etc.)
- Paintbrush
- 2 sheets of white paper

Plan of Attack
You may take for granted that if you need to jot a note down or finish a homework assignment you can just grab a piece of paper and start writing. But the story behind how paper is made is a little more complicated.

Pulp papermaking is believed to have been invented in China in the year 2 CE. The Chinese invented this new substance to write on because writing on silk was very expensive. Although today we think of paper as being made from trees, paper can be made from many different sources, such as grasses or even cotton.

How is paper made from trees? To make paper from wood, the wood must first be broken down into pulp. Wood is formed of many different fibers called *cellulose*. These cellulose fibers are held together by a substance called *lignin*. Lignin is like a glue that helps make wood so sturdy. One way to break down the wood into pulp is to use chemicals to separate the lignin out of the wood and then grind up the cellulose that is left to make pulp. The other way is to make the pulp out of *both* the lignin and cellulose by heating the wood up with steam.

The amazing thing about lignin is that it is the key to why some paper, like newspaper, turns yellow. Lignin can undergo something called oxidation by the oxygen in the air all around us. Oxidation happens when the lignin molecules in paper are exposed to oxygen and become unstable. This process changes the structure of the lignin and makes it possible for the lignin to absorb more light.

When paper absorbs more light, it ends up looking darker. So a newspaper that has lignin in it, over time, will change color. As you might guess, the *oxidation* process does not happen overnight. We probably don't want to wait months or years to watch the lignin in the paper oxidize and discolor the paper, so we are going to fast-forward Mother Nature a bit and watch the oxidization process happen before our very eyes!

✳ ***Very Important!*** *Because this mission involves using chemicals, you need to have a parent or responsible adult do this activity with you.*

1. Take 2 pads of fine steel wool and place them in a sealable container. Try to use a container you (and your family) are OK with throwing away after this experiment is over.

2. Next, pour in 16 ounces of distilled white vinegar. Seal the container tightly and leave it for at least one week. The acid from the vinegar will oxidize the steel wool. This is similar to how the lignin in the paper oxidizes over time.

3. Use a paintbrush to lightly smear the oxidized solution over a couple of sheets of white paper. Instead of waiting for the paper's lignin to age and oxidize, we are applying an already oxidized solution directly to the paper. This oxidized solution will turn regular white paper into something similar to that treasure chest map!

Take It to the Max!

The oxidation of the steel wool from this experiment is the first step in a process you are probably already aware of: rusting. This can be a huge problem for cars in some states, while not much of an issue in others. Do some research and try to find out why some people would rather buy a car from Arizona or New Mexico over Florida or New York.

PART V

SOCIAL STUDIES

GO WEST! THE AMERICAN PIONEER

Content Area: Social Studies
Primary Skills Focus: Historical Inquiry

Mission Objective: Churn through the world of the Oregon Trail, Daniel Boone, and the Trail of Tears. Along the way you will learn how butter was made the pioneer way.

Look at a US map from the mid-1800s and compare it to your map today. You will notice some similarities, but also some big differences.

A current map of the United States shows formed states from coast to coast. But the United States was not always like this. The majority of our country's first immigrants came from Europe and arrived in the northeastern part of the country. How and why did people move west to make states like California? In the 1800s people didn't travel in cars; how did they get from one coast to the other? Can you imagine all the difficulties of traveling up to 2,000 miles across the country, in all weather conditions?

American pioneers settled in the United States as they moved west, but what about the people who were already living there? You are going to become a westward traveler and find out the good and the bad of the pioneer life.

Learning the Lingo

American pioneers: A name for the group of people in American history who moved west to claim, settle, and develop new land. Since no European settlers had gone to many of these places before, they either ignored or did not understand that much of the land they wanted to claim already had Native people living there.

Homestead Act: A law signed by President Abraham Lincoln in 1862 that encouraged people to colonize undeveloped land owned by the government. This land was west of the Mississippi River. People who applied for the land had to live on it for five years and make improvements, and then they could own it forever. Although the land was claimed by the US government before the homesteaders moved onto it, there were already Native people living on much of this land before the new American settlers came to it.

Oregon Trail: A 2,000-mile route across the United States from the Missouri River to Oregon that people traveled on to go west. This route was popular in the mid-1800s. The trail started before railroad tracks were built through this area so people traveled on it by wagon, horse, or even walked. To continue along the trail many families had to try to cross rivers with all their belongings. They had to make repairs to their wagons, deal with lack of food, fight illness, and risk fighting with Native Americans living in the area.

Emigrant party on the road to California, 1850. *Library of Congress LC-DIG-ppmsca-02887*

Materials

- Heavy or whipping cream (1.25 ounces per batch)
- Baby food jar with lid
- Spoon or dull knife
- Cheese cloth or kitchen towel
- Salt (to taste; optional)

Plan of Attack

The American pioneer had to go through a lot to achieve the dream of making a home in the unsettled territory of the United States. Traveling the Oregon Trail was not for the faint of heart. Many people who traveled to settle out west didn't make it and perished along the way. You may be wondering what made it so hard.

Remember, many of the modern conveniences we have today did not exist on the trail. People used wagons and oxen to travel, and there were no refrigerators to keep food from spoiling. They could carry only food that would not spoil too quickly. Because their oxen had to pull all the weight of the wagon, the pioneers could not bring a lot of extra, heavy items either. The pioneers were at times moving through already settled Native land, and sometimes the different groups would attack each other along the way. The weather and geography were difficult; all the travelers had for heat and shelter were wood fires and tents.

Traveling and daily activities in the 1800s were much harder than they are today. Could you have made it on the Oregon Trail? You are about to find out by making your own food, much like the American pioneer would have.

1. Prepare your whipping cream or heavy cream by taking it from fridge and letting it get close to room temperature. Getting the cream to room temperature will mean less time shaking when preparing your butter.

2. Make sure the baby food jar you choose is clean; wash it out with soap and water if needed. Make sure to rinse all soap out of the jar prior to starting to make your butter.

3. Fill jar halfway with cream.

4. Place lid on jar tightly so it does not come off. (Adult: please help by making sure the lid is on tightly and that the area is clear for shaking the jar.)

5. Shake jar with cream up and down for 10 to 15 minutes. You will know that you are almost done shaking when a lot of the liquid is gone away.

6. Once a lot of the liquid is gone, you should see some solid butter in the jar. Take off the lid and scoop out solid butter with a spoon or dull knife.

7. Put your butter on a cheesecloth or towel, and squeeze to get all the excess liquid out from your butter.

8. Put the butter in a container and place it in the fridge for one hour to help it become harder. (You can add a pinch of salt to the butter if desired after it gets firm in the fridge.)

9. You can now use your homemade butter! (It is fresh butter so use within a week.)

10. The pioneers made butter in a similar way to this, but they didn't have the option of using the fridge to make it harder or to keep it from spoiling. Can you see now how hard some activities of daily pioneer life must have been?

Take It to the Max!

Did you know that before there were travelers on the Oregon Trail there were explorers who mapped out a way to travel across the United States to the Pacific Ocean? Find out who Lewis and Clark were and how their exploration changed America.

GLOBALIZATION: HOW THE WORLD IS CONNECTED

Content Focus: Social Studies
Primary Skills Focus: Exploring Connections

Mission Objective: Uncover how the world is becoming more and more interconnected, track where many of your household items are produced, and then take a stance on globalization.

Many years ago, most of the things Americans bought and used were made right here in United States. Over the years, however, companies have started looking to other countries to produce our consumer goods because the people in the other countries will work for a much lower wage. As a result of producing goods like sneakers and radios for a lower cost, companies were able to sell the goods cheaper to us (the consumer), in the end making more profit for the company. This process of economic relationships between companies in different countries is called *globalization*.

Some say globalization is a great thing because it raises the standard of living in poorer countries by providing manufacturing jobs and increases the American standard of living by making items less expensive for us to buy. Other people, however, see globalization as a bad thing. They say that companies take away American jobs and give them to people overseas. Many factories in places like Michigan and Ohio have closed and people have lost their jobs because it is simply so much cheaper for these companies to manufacture their goods in other countries. Some opponents of globalization also say that the environment is becoming polluted because countries with a lot of factories (like China) don't have the same environmental laws as the United States. As a result, Chinese factories are allowed to emit more smoke and fumes in the air than American factories. Other issues that people have with globalization are that some countries have unsafe working conditions for their workers, don't pay a fair wage, and even let kids work in their factories. In this mission you will take on the role of a United Nations economist and help decide whether globalization is a good thing for America and the world.

Learning the Lingo

consumer: A person who buys and uses goods and services.
disposable income: Extra money left over after you have paid for your living expenses (housing, food, etc.) that you are free to spend on whatever you want.
globalization: An ongoing process in which different countries and companies are coming together and increasing the exchange of money, services, and ideas.

standard of living: This is the level of material comfort a person or group has. Oftentimes this is measured by money, education, or level of health care.

United Nations: A group of countries that meet together to discuss and make decisions about the world.

Materials

- Paper and writing utensil
- 15 portable items from around the home (such as a clock, MP3 player, T-shirt, etc.)
- Copy or printout of a world map
- 15 small dot stickers

Plan of Attack

First, you will complete the following T-chart by finding 15 items around your house and looking at the label to determine where it was made. On the left side of the chart, write down what the item is. On the right side, write down the country where your item was made.

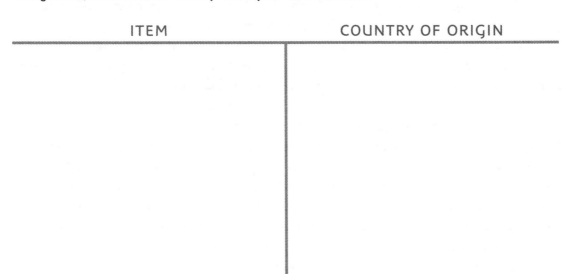

ITEM	COUNTRY OF ORIGIN

Next, for each item, place a dot sticker on your world map in the country where it was produced. You may have to use an atlas to figure out where all the countries are. Most likely, you have a lot of dots in the continent of Asia. This will give you a clearer picture of where most of the world's factories are located.

Finally, you will take on the role of an economist and write a letter to the United Nations (a collection of different countries that make world decisions) urging them to either keep going with the trend of globalization or to stop it. Be sure to give specific reasons for your decision. Your reasons don't have to just come from this mission; you can use outside resources or come up with your own. Use the Brain Buster questions below to help you come up with good ideas and find resources to help you write a great letter about globalization.

Brain Buster Questions

1. What reasons would a company have for moving its factory from the United States to another country, such as Vietnam or Guatemala? (Hint: One thing to think about is the difference in average worker wages in each country.)

2. Can you think of any reasons that somebody would not want a factory or business to move to their country or hometown?

3. What is the biggest problem, from your point of view, with the United States losing jobs to other countries?

Take It to the Max!

Many towns and cities house factories that manufacture, or create, items that people use every day. Things like Cabbage Patch Kids, Big Wheels, Nalgene water bottles, and Louisville Slugger bats are all made in America. Find out if your town has a factory. Oftentimes, you can set up a time to tour the factory and see how all of these items are made. Find out what the people that work at the factory think about globalization and the manufacturing of goods in other countries.

THE SONGS OF THE WIND: NATIVE AMERICAN RELIGIOUS TRADITION

Content Area: Social Studies
Primary Skills Focus: Historical Inquiry

Mission Objective: Get an overview of Native American religious history and create a dreamcatcher.

When the new settlers arrived in America, some were surprised to find that there were already people living in "the new world." The explorer Christopher Columbus was trying to reach the country of India, and so he called the people he saw "Indians." We know now that the people early explorers called "Indians" were actually Native Americans who were already living on the land that would become the United States.

The new settlers to America had many differences with the Native Americans. Many of the settlers thought the native people didn't have a religion; they wanted to share with, and even force their religion on the native people. These immigrants spread Christianity, and some Native people adopted Christianity as their religion and continue it even today.

Did you know that the Native Americans, who are composed of many different tribes, have many unique and interesting spiritual and religious traditions? Do you realize that people are still practicing many of these traditions today?

You are about to be introduced to practices and beliefs of some Native Americans by learning about some of these traditions.

Learning the Lingo

American Indian Religious Freedom Act: A US law passed in 1978 that gave protection to the religious rights and cultures of American Indians, Aleuts, Eskimos, and Native Hawaiians. Included in this law was protection for these groups to have access to sacred sites. To many of these groups there are certain natural sites that are sacred, and these were finally protected.

bawaajige nagwaagan: This is the word for an object known as a "dream catcher" in the language of a Native American tribe known as the Ojibwa. The dream catcher is a wooden hoop, inside of which a threadlike material is used to make a pattern that looks similar to a spider web. The Ojibwa believe that the dream catcher will help filter out bad dreams and only let the good dreams get to the person sleeping.

pantheism: A view, or way of thinking, that sees the universe or nature as being identical to God. In this view, nature is a sacred thing. Many Native American religious beliefs fall within the views of pantheism.

religion: Sometimes described as faith or a belief system, a religion is usually more organized than what our personal beliefs are. In religions there may be a public, organized time and place to pray, like going to a church, synagogue, or mosque.

spirituality: A word that is defined differently by many people. You can think of spirituality as a path that people use to understand and find meaning and value in their life. Many people believe you can be spiritual and religious at the same time, or that you can be one without necessarily being the other.

Materials

- 2–3 bird feathers (natural or artificial feathers are available at craft or hobby stores)
- Spool of thin yarn or string of any color
- Circular wooden or metal hoop (such as an embroidery hoop), or a long, bendable wooden twig (such as a grapevine or willow branch), or any circular object that has space in the middle (a round plastic lid with the middle cut out will work). Whatever you use, the hole should be about the size of an adult palm or just bigger.
- Scissors
- Water and twist ties (if using wooden twig)
- Beads (optional)

Plan of Attack

Because different Native American people, or tribes, have different cultures and spiritual beliefs, there is no singular Native American religion or religious tradition. For thousands of years there have been many different Native American tribes, some living far away from each other. Since they were not all living together, we should expect that there are different languages, cultures, and religions.

There are similarities between many Native American, or American Indian, religious beliefs and practices. In general, many Native American religious beliefs hold a strong connection to that land on which they live, or lived. This land is considered sacred, and most of these religious traditions are not separate from daily living. It is so hard to separate these religious traditions from daily life and actions that many Native people do not even consider it religion but more a spirituality or culture.

It has not always been easy for Native people to practice their religions freely. Many of the cultural practices or traditions were never taught to outsiders, and many of the first settlers to America did not understand that there were Native American religions.

In fact, some of the new settlers thought the Native people had no religious beliefs and tried to get them to give up their culture and customs and convert to other beliefs. Many children who belonged to Native cultures were sent to boarding schools where they were not allowed to continue to learn their own languages or cultures. Some people believe that one reason for these schools was to help destroy the religious beliefs and customs of the Native people.

Even though some people do not realize it, descendants of the Native Americans, and others, are still practicing Native American culture, customs, and religious traditions. Although there are many, many different cultures and customs (depending on which group you are associated with), there have been some traditions that are practiced by many different groups.

One of the traditions that has been accepted by many different Native people is the use of something called *bawaajige nagwaagan*, or the dream catcher, that originated with the people of the Ojibwa Nation. As you learned before, a dream catcher is a tool that is used to help catch or trap bad dreams to protect the person who is sleeping. The dreams get trapped in the web that is formed by string inside a wooden loop. The web, like a spider web, lets the sun shine through it and burn up the bad dreams so they no longer exist in the morning.

You now have a chance to make a dream catcher of your own and show your unity and understanding of Native American culture and practices.

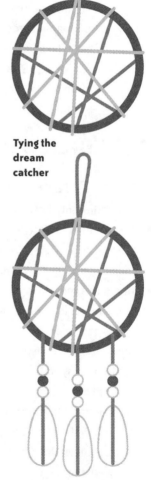

Tying the dream catcher

1. If using a wooden twig or grapevine, complete this step first. Otherwise begin with step 2. Place the twig or grapevine in water until it is soft enough that it can be bent into a circle. (This may take several hours depending on thickness.) Use the twist-tie to secure the ends in making a complete circle. Then wrap the yarn or string multiple times around where the ends meet and tie tightly to make sure your circle hoop will not come apart (you can remove twist tie after yarn has secured the loop).

2. Tie yarn to one end of the circle hoop, cross the circle with the yarn, and loop it around the opposite edge. Continue this until there are many lines of yarn across the circle of the loop.

3. After finishing these loops across, you can make a spider web–like pattern in the middle by weaving the yarn in a circular pattern.

4. Remember, each dream catcher is unique, so your pattern does not need to look like the one pictured here or like any other dream catcher.

5. Cut several 3-inch pieces of yarn. Tie one end of each to the bottom of the dream catcher and decorate the other ends by stringing beads or tying on bird feathers or both, so that they dangle below the hoop. Add as many beads or feathers as you would like.

Tie a piece of yarn to the top to use for hanging.

Take It to the Max!

You now know about one creation that has special meaning to many Native people. Can you think of any other items that Native Americans created to express themselves? You get one hint: these objects can be large and made from wood.

DEMOCRACY! WHAT'S YOUR VOTE?

Content Focus: Social Studies
Primary Skills Focus: Investigating and Classifying

Mission Objective: Learn about the evolution of democratic systems around the world and then research democratically elected officials in your area.

What do you think of when you hear the word *election*? Do you think of freedom, democracy, and how amazing it is that we, the normal people, get to choose our laws and leaders? Probably not. You may think of annoying commercials and long lines your parents have to stand in to vote, and you may not even care who is elected. That is totally understandable. Sometimes, when something is so normal (like the ability to vote) we can forget how special it really is.

The idea that common people can choose their leaders is actually a pretty new idea. For the vast majority of human history it was the richest people with the biggest armies that ruled over everyone and got to make the laws. Whether it was a king or queen in Old England, an emperor or empress in China, or the Sapa Inca in the Americas, most rulers were *monarchs*, or leaders of a form of government where the power rests with one person. An exception to this was the Ancient Greeks, who did have a form of democracy. A democracy is a government where the power is in the hands of the people, not a monarch.

When monarchs were in power they could normally do whatever they wanted. If they didn't like someone, they could have that person killed. If they wanted a farmer's crops, they would just use their army to take it. Then, in the late 1600s, a philosopher named John Locke came up with the idea of "the consent of the governed." Consent is another word for permission. This was the idea that it wasn't the king or queen who had the absolute authority to rule given by God, as had been believed, but it was the people that gave rulers that power by obeying them. This meant that it was the people that had the power, not the ruler.

This was one of the reasons the American colonists split from Great Britain and fought the Revolutionary War in 1776. Some colonists wanted a greater say and more representation in their current government and others did not want to live under the laws of King George III. They were being forced to pay taxes and obey laws that they didn't get to help create and objected to what they called "taxation without representation."

After the colonists won the Revolutionary War, they set up a system of government that is still in place today, in which the people get to vote for leaders who must have the best interests of the common people in mind if they want to stay in power. Americans have the ability to peacefully unseat their leaders if they don't like their ideas and actions. There are other countries—including Costa Rica, Iceland, Japan, and many others—that have democracy and choose their own leaders in elections.

An interesting fact is how few Americans actually vote. Among people that have the ability to vote (18 years or older, registered in their county, etc.) only about 65 percent vote in presidential elections. That means only two out of three people that could have a voice in shaping our country take the time to do so. In this mission you are going to find out who shapes the laws *you* live under and what powers they have.

Learning the Lingo

consent of the governed: This is the idea that the power of kings and queens, emperors and empresses, and other monarchs comes from the people. The rulers only have power because the people give it to them. This was a radical idea at the time because most monarchs thought that their power came from God.

democracy: In a democracy, the people have the power to vote and make decisions about how their government should run. There are two types of democracy:

• **direct democracy:** Every law or decision is directly voted on by the people (very few countries have this).

• **representative democracy:** People vote in representatives who then vote on laws and decisions in the interest of the people (this is what we have in America).

monarchy: In a monarchy one person holds all the power over a country. This title (king, queen, emperor, empress, sultan, etc.) is usually hereditary. This means it is passed from parent to child.

Plan of Attack

You are now going to find out who is in power and what they actually do. For each of the positions on page 106, write in the name of the person who holds that position and what that position does. What are their day-to-day duties? You can get this information in a few different ways. One of the easiest may be the Internet. Because these positions are not all under the same level of government (city, county, state, or federal) you may have to visit different websites for the city, state, and county you live in. Another way is to go to your city hall or county offices and ask around. While you may not get to speak with the officials yourself, you can talk to someone who can answer your questions. You can also call these offices and ask your questions. You can also go to your local library and ask the librarian to help you research. Good Luck!

Take It to the Max!

Set up an interview with an elected official to find out what life in government is really like. It's OK to call them and ask for an interview. The interview can be over the phone or in their office. You can ask them questions like:

- Why did you go into politics?
- What is it like working in government?
- What are your main goals for this term?
- What is important for kids to know about how the government works?

FEDERAL (US NATIONAL GOVERNMENT)

★ PRESIDENT

Name:

Duties:

★ SENATOR FOR YOUR DISTRICT

Name:

Duties:

★ REPRESENTATIVE FOR YOUR DISTRICT

Name:

Duties:

STATE

★ GOVERNOR

Name:

Duties:

★ STATE SENATOR FOR YOUR DISTRICT

Name:

Duties:

★ STATE REPRESENTATIVE FOR YOUR DISTRICT

Name:

Duties:

COUNTY

★COUNTY COMMISSIONER

Name:

Duties:

★ SHERIFF

Name:

Duties:

CITY/TOWN

★ MAYOR

Name:

Duties:

★ CITY/TOWN COUNCIL MEMBER FOR YOUR DISTRICT

Name:

Duties:

ROCK THE VOTE BY "ROCKING THE BOAT"?

Content Area: Social Studies
Primary Skills Focus: Historical Inquiry

Mission Objective: Navigate the complex historical journey of voting in the United States. You will test your voting IQ by using your newfound knowledge.

Have you ever heard somebody say, "it is my right as an American . . . " when they were talking about politics or the government? As a US citizen one of the rights that you have when you turn 18 years old is the right to vote. The right to vote carries a lot of power because it can help decide who runs our government in the future. Voting helps each citizen have a voice in helping to shape the United States.

Believe it or not, even though it seems simple, the process of voting can be complicated. Did you know that at one point in time women and African Americans were not allowed to vote in the United States? You are going to go back in time to learn about some of the history of voting in America, such as the women's suffrage movement and the Voting Rights Act. You will also see how voting works today, and see if you can correctly predict the outcome of a special election scenario!

Learning the Lingo

Electoral College: This can be confusing because it is not a college at all. This is a process in which we elect the president and vice-president in America. The Electoral College is made up of 538 "electors" who are chosen to pledge their vote to the presidential candidate that voters in their state wish to elect. The number of electors per state is based on population: the more people that live in a state, the more electors they will have. If a candidate receives more than 50 percent of the popular vote, he or she gets all of that state's electoral votes. A presidential candidate has to win the majority (270) of the votes from these electors to become president.

popular vote: This is the number of individual votes a candidate received in an election.

Voting Rights Act: A law passed by the government in 1965 to make sure that people in the United States did actually have an equal right, or opportunity, to vote. Prior to this act, there were laws and rules in place that made it hard for certain people, such as African Americans, to vote.

women's suffrage: The right of women to vote and run for political office. It sounds confusing because the word "suffrage" may sound like "suffering," but suffrage is simply the right to vote.

Materials

- Paper and writing utensil

Plan of Attack

You may take it for granted that every adult has the right to vote because you have heard your parent, teacher, or even neighbor talk about voting in a recent election. But that has not always been the case. In 1787 when the Constitution of the United States was passed, it only gave white male property owners who were at least 21 years of age the right to vote. For almost the next 100 years, only white men could participate in Election Day.

In 1870, however, the 15th Amendment (an amendment is a change to the constitution) was passed that gave all men, regardless of race or ethnicity, the right to vote. This was a big change for voting in the United States because at this point, legally, former slaves and all African American men now had the right to vote. There were still a few problems, however: First, women of any race still did not have the right to vote. Second, there were no laws prohibiting people from making it hard for African American men to successfully vote even though they had the legal right.

In the early to mid-1800s the movement for women's suffrage started to take hold in the United States. The women's suffrage movement was aimed at gaining women the right to vote and stand for elected office. By 1890 the National American Women Suffrage Association was formed and lead by prominent suffragists (women seeking the right to vote) like Susan B. Anthony, Elizabeth Cady Stanton, and Lucy Stone. The suffragists used lawsuits, protests, and signature campaigns to try to obtain the right to vote.

One of the most effective ways for them to gain public awareness for their cause was to go ahead and try to vote in an election. Susan B. Anthony was arrested for illegally voting. She was put on trial and even found guilty, but her actions led to a lot of exposure and publicity for the suffragists' cause. Eventually their tactics worked and in 1920 the 19th Amendment was passed, giving women 21 and older the right to vote.

During the next 30 to 40 years it became clear that blacks and other minorities in some parts of the United States were being prevented from voting through the use of tactics that were not clearly stated as being illegal in the 15th Amendment. Minorities faced high voting taxes, tests to prove literacy (ability to read), and threats and bullying so they would not vote. In response to these harassments, the Voting Rights Act was passed in 1965 to specifically make these behaviors illegal and make the 15th Amendment meaningful again.

Now that you know some of the history of voting, and how lucky US citizens are to have the right to vote freely with no threats of being bullied or scared, it is time to test your knowledge of how voting works today!

We know that most adult citizens can cast a vote for president and when the votes are all counted, that makes up the popular vote. We also know that to become elected, the president has to win the Electoral College, which takes a majority of the electoral votes. So let's see if you can predict the winner of a special presidential election scenario.

1. There are two US presidential candidates: Karen and Sharon.

2. Analyze the mock presidential results below. Remember, if a candidate wins over 50 percent of the popular votes, she receives all of that state's electoral votes. While these are fictitious (made-up) states, they do represent real states in the United States.

Mock Presidential Election Results

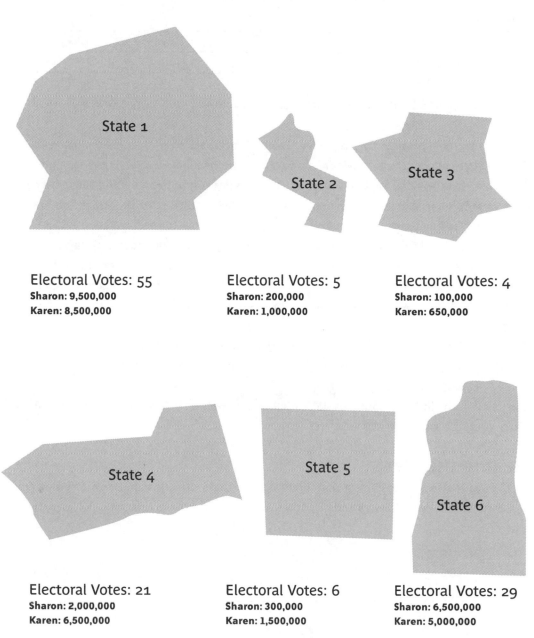

Electoral Votes: 55
Sharon: 9,500,000
Karen: 8,500,000

Electoral Votes: 5
Sharon: 200,000
Karen: 1,000,000

Electoral Votes: 4
Sharon: 100,000
Karen: 650,000

Electoral Votes: 21
Sharon: 2,000,000
Karen: 6,500,000

Electoral Votes: 6
Sharon: 300,000
Karen: 1,500,000

Electoral Votes: 29
Sharon: 6,500,000
Karen: 5,000,000

To help you in figuring who is the next president of the United States, Karen or Sharon, try to answer the next few questions.

1. Who won the popular vote?

	Sharon	Karen
Popular Vote (total # of votes)		

2. Who won the electoral vote?

	Sharon	Karen
# of Electoral Votes		

3. Can you win the popular vote and not the electoral vote?

Sharon is the new president of the United States. Remember, to win the presidential election in the United States you must win a majority of votes from the Electoral College. It does not matter that more people actually voted for Karen, who won the popular vote with over 4,000,000 more people actually voting for her. You *can* win the popular vote and still not be elected president. This has actually happened four times in our nation's history. Does this seem fair to you?

Furthermore, this election simulation also shows how important more populous states are in our elections. Did you notice that Sharon (the winner) won only two states? But, since those states had the most people (and therefore the most electoral votes) it didn't matter that Karen won the other four. While these states were fictitious, their numbers of voters and electoral votes were based on real states:

1. CALIFORNIA   **2.** WEST VIRGINIA **3.** IDAHO

4. PENNSYLVANIA **5.** MISSISSIPPI   **6** NEW YORK

Can you see why the most populous states (California, Texas, New York, Florida, etc.) are so important to presidential candidates?

Take It to the Max!

Did you know that prisoners in most states in the United States have lost their right to vote? With a little detective work see if you can find out if there are any states where prisoners still have the right to vote.

HOW MUCH OF THE STORY ARE YOU GETTING? BIAS IN THE MEDIA

Content Focus: Social Studies
Primary Skills Focus: Investigating and Classifying

Mission Objective: Get information on how the messages we receive from the media are heavily influenced by the way they are delivered. Then, use this knowledge to try to identify bias in current news stories.

We all have certain biases in almost everything we do. Bias is our tendency to like, or prefer, one thing over another. You may be biased toward chocolate ice cream over vanilla, football over basketball, or cats over dogs. While biases are natural, the goal of news reporters is to report the news impartially (without bias). They are supposed to report only the facts but oftentimes they insert their own views into the stories. This happens a lot with politics. One reporter will favor one side, or politician, over another and try to sway you to agree with him or her without coming out and saying it.

One example of this was when the United States started sending troops to Iraq in the early 2000s. One news agency's headline read, U.S. Starts Invasion of Iraq while another read, The U.S. Begins Liberation of Iraq. Even though these two stories were on the same topic, the word choices (invasion versus liberation) were meant to sway our thinking about what the United States was doing. In this activity you will use the Learning the Lingo section to become an expert in detecting bias and then spot the bias in stories you (or your family) read every day.

Learning the Lingo

bias by coverage: How much coverage one story gets versus another is another indicator of bias. If a president makes a mistake and one newspaper or website hardly mentions it (or sticks it in the back of the paper or the bottom of the webpage) they are probably fans of the president and don't want to embarrass that person. Conversely, if another newspaper or website blows everything that a particular president does out of proportion and turns all blunders into headline news, they are probably against that president.

bias by experts: Often reporters will refer to people in their stories as "experts." Whether reporting on an airplane crash and bringing in an aviation "expert" or a financial story that involves a business "expert," having someone that they can refer to as an "expert" seems to add authority and credibility to their story. But, who are these experts? What does it take to be called an "expert"? Education? Experience? Often, these experts are not neutral but work for a company or government organization trying to push one view.

bias by title: Just like the Iraq example above, how a reporter titles a story sets the tone and can sway people to think one way or another. There is a big difference between titling an article, "Firefighters Able to Save 12 Houses from Blaze" vs. "Firefighters Let 26 Houses Burn" even though these titles may refer to the same event. Pay attention to the titles; they are very telling about what the reporter thinks.

Materials

- Paper and writing utensil
- Two news stories reporting the same event

Plan of Attack

There is bias in almost every news article you read and watch. Most news agencies try to stay neutral, but people's opinions show themselves in many ways. You are to find two newspapers or web pages that are reporting the same story. Try to find something controversial like politics, the economy, or war. You will read both articles and look for the types of bias listed in the "Lingo" section. Try to figure out what side the reporter is on.

1. Are they saying only good things about this person/event? Only bad?

2. Do the article titles reveal any clues about the reporter's opinion?

3. Are they leaving out certain information?

4. Who are their "experts"? Research these experts on your own. Do they work for certain companies that have a stake in the story? Have they worked for politicians before?

5. Does one website have the story on the top of the page in big, bold letters while the other has it as a small link on the bottom?

What kind of biases were you able to identify? Have a conversation with an older family member about the two stories and tell them what you found.

Take It to the Max!

The next time someone tells you a story about a disagreement, or fight, try to find the bias in his or her story. Are they leaving out details? Are they exaggerating? Are they trying to get you on their side? Think about how much bias can affect someone's story when they get in trouble with a parent or teacher. Bias detection can be a very powerful tool in life.

THIS LAND IS MY LAND, THIS LAND IS YOUR LAND: THE BLACK HILLS TREATY

Content Focus: Social Studies
Primary Skills Focus: Historical Inquiry

Mission Objective: Find out about Native American history and take on the role of a government consultant tasked with resolving a land rights issue.

While most people will tell you that Christopher Columbus or the Vikings discovered America, others would say that the Americas were discovered by Native Americans that crossed a land bridge between Russia and Alaska sometime around 12,000 to 25,000 years ago. European explorers and settlers began coming to North America in the 15th century (1400s) and didn't stop. By the 18th century (1700s) the descendants of these early settlers had created a new country, the United States of America. Many Americans believed in what they called *Manifest Destiny*.

Manifest Destiny was a national belief that the United States was destined to spread from the Atlantic Ocean to the Pacific Ocean. People believed that it had been religiously proclaimed that America (mostly Anglo-Saxon whites) would spread its culture and way of life and take over the land and people (mostly Native Americans and non-whites) that spread out West across the continent. The picture below, *American Progress* painted by John Gast in 1872, shows the sentiment of the time period. Before you read further, see how many clues you can find that tell you that this painting is about Manifest Destiny.

Did you notice that the Americans (represented by the settlers) are marching together from East to West, driving out the Native Americans and buffalo? Did you notice that an angel-like figure hovers above them, *guiding* them across the continent? Did you notice the power lines and railroads—representing progress—that follow the Americans? This image sets the scene for your mission, in which you will see what happens when these different cultural groups clash.

Learning the Lingo

impoverished: Being very poor or deprived. Having very little money to buy the essentials of life (heat, housing, food, etc.)

manifest destiny: A national belief that the United States was destined to spread across the continent from the Atlantic Ocean to the Pacific Ocean.

reservation: A piece of land set aside for Native Americans by the US government.

treaty: A formal agreement between two states, nations, or government organizations.

American Progress, 1872. *Library of Congress LC-DIG-ppmsca-09855*

Materials

- Paper and writing utensil

Plan of Attack

When Americans would come in contact with native tribes, they would often try to make treaties with them. In these treaties the Native Americans would usually be guaranteed a specific piece of land in exchange for giving Americans something they wanted. One of these places was the Black Hills of South Dakota and Wyoming.

The Black Hills are a small mountain range coming up from the flat grassland in the Northern United States. By the mid-1800s the Lakota had lived in the Black Hills for generations and had been fighting the US army to keep their land. After years of fighting, the US government signed the Treaty of Fort Laramie that guaranteed land ownership of the Black Hills to the Lakota in 1868. Less than a decade later, gold was discovered in the Black Hills and miners and settlers came pouring into the tribe's territory.

The US government initially tried to stop its citizens from trespassing into this region guaranteed to the Lakota. In the end, the government gave in to the miners' demands and sent army troops to establish posts in an effort to force the Native Americans out of the Black Hills. By 1877 the army had taken control of the land militarily and forced the natives to give it to the government. The US officials

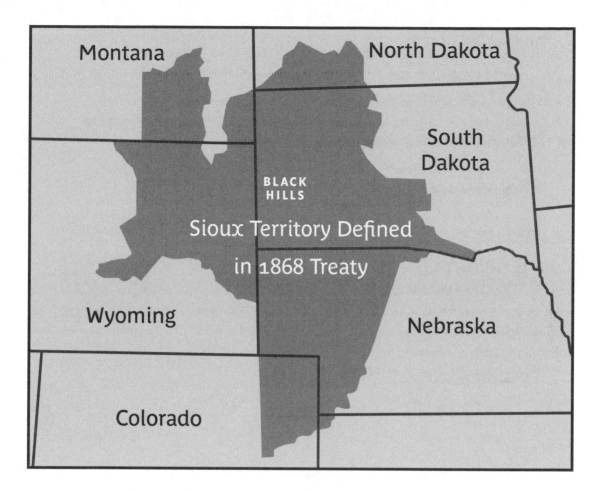

broke their promises and treaty because of an uncontrollable greed for the gold believed to be in the Black Hills. This fighting and land theft destroyed much of the Lakota's unity and strength as a people. Today, many of these native descendants live on the Pine Ridge Indian Reservation, about 100 miles southeast of their former homeland. The reservation is a very poor community with high unemployment, where many Native Americans struggle to pay for things like food and heat. In 1980 the Supreme Court saw that this land theft was wrong and decided the tribes should be compensated $106 million, the 1877 land value of $17.5 million plus interest. The court officially determined that our government's "taking of tribal property" was not right. The Lakota refused payment, stating that if they accepted, they would be acknowledging US ownership of the Black Hills. Instead, the Lakota want their land back. The money allocated to the tribes (the $106 million from 1980) has been sitting in an interest-bearing account and is now worth more than $500 million. Still, the impoverished Lakota refuse to take it.

You are a special land-rights consultant that has been brought in to decide what to do here. You must write a letter to the Secretary of the Interior (a government official who deals with cultural and tribal issues) that includes your position on the following questions:

1. First, should the US government give the Black Hills back to the Lakota? Since the government has acknowledged that the taking of the Black Hills was illegal, does it have an obligation to give that land back to the Lakota if they want it?

2. If the government does give the Black Hills back, what then happens to all the Americans that currently live in them? Do they now get money for being forced off their property? If so, who will pay it?

3. If the government doesn't give the land back, does it have an obligation to help improve life on the reservation?

If you wish, you can look up the address for the Secretary of the Interior and send this letter.

Take It to the Max!

Many areas across the United States have fascinating stories about Native Americans who once lived there. Do some research on Native American tribes in or around your town. Who were they? What was their culture like? What happened to them? Are they still around? The story of how natives and settlers interacted varies around the country. How is the history of Native Americans near you similar or different to that of the Lakota of the Black Hills?

THE FABRIC OF AMERICA: IMMIGRATION

Content Area: Social Studies
Primary Skills Focus: Historical Inquiry

Mission Objective: Discover how immigrants have helped shape America and then either explore your own immigration history or interview an immigrant in your community to discuss his or her experiences.

One of the things that makes America so cool is that everyone's ancestors are from somewhere else. Did you know that even Native Americans moved here from somewhere else? Scientists believe that Native Americans crossed a land bridge called Beringia between present-day Russia and Alaska sometime between 12,000 and 25,000 years ago. That land bridge was exposed because the planet was in an Ice Age and all the water that usually covered the land was frozen up in ice and snow. It took thousands of years but these people soon spread from the top of North America all the way down to the bottom tip of South America. Explorers from Europe showed up around 500 years ago, and the word spread about this beautiful land, full of opportunities.

People from all over the world started immigrating to America in search of a better life. Some people came for higher-paying jobs, some for cheap farmland, and others came for adventure. Some people still come to America for the same reasons. These people are called *immigrants*. In this activity you will be learning firsthand about the immigrant experience.

Learning the Lingo

Beringia: The land bridge used by native peoples thousands of years ago to cross from Asia to North America.

immigrate: To migrate or move to another country.

pull-factors: The reasons a person chooses to move to a specific country. What *pulled* them to America over other countries?

push-factors: The reasons people choose to leave their home countries. What *pushed* them into leaving?

Materials
- Paper and writing utensil

Plan of Attack

You have two options:

OPTION A

Everyone's family immigrated to America at one point in time. Your mission is to find out the story of your own family's immigration experience. Somewhere along the way somebody from your family made his or her way to America. Maybe it was your parents? Your grandma? Your great-great-great grandpa? You're going to interview a family member and get the details about this person or people:

1.   What country were they from?

2.   Why did they leave their home? (push-factors)

3.   Why did they choose America? (pull-factors)

4.   What was the experience like coming over? Did they take a boat? A plane?

5.   Where did they settle in America?

6.   What kind of jobs did they do?

7.   How was American life different than life where they came from?

Don't worry if you can't get all this information. These are just questions to get you started. If you are having trouble with this, there are many online tools that may help, including immigration records, ancestry websites, and government census records. Feel free to make up your own questions, too. In some families it may be hard to find this information. If that's the case, you should try Option B.

OPTION B

Thousands of people are still immigrating to America every year. You probably know some. Your job is to interview someone who immigrated to America and find out about their life. You may have to ask around to find someone who moved here from another country. Maybe it's your barber? Or someone your mom works with? Your friend's dad? Find someone who was born in another country and ask him or her the following questions:

1.   What country are they from?

2.   Why did they leave their home? (push-factor)

3.   Why did they choose America? (pull-factor)

4.   What was the experience like coming over? Did they take a boat? A plane?

5.   Where did they settle in America?

6. What kind of jobs have they done?

7. How is American life different than life where they came from?

8. What advice would they give new immigrants?

Take It to the Max!

Immigration is in the news all the time. Many people have strong views about whether the United States should accept new immigrants and how they should be treated once they're here. Next time you notice a story on immigration (either on TV, online, or in a newspaper) pay attention and discuss it with your family.

PART VI

BIOLOGY

WHEN NIGHTTIME IS THE RIGHT TIME: NOCTURNAL ADAPTATIONS

Content Focus: Biology
Primary Skill Focus: Exploring Connections

Mission Objective: Explore different adaptations animals make to live and hunt in the dark. Then, engage in two simulations where you "see" these adaptations in action.

Did you know that some animals live their lives in the dark? These animals are called *nocturnal*. Animals that are active during the day are called *diurnal*. What makes nighttime animals successful is the adaptations that they have developed over thousands of years that give them the tools to get around and find food at night. In this mission you will learn about a couple of these adaptations—night vision and echolocation—and will test your skills to see if you have what it takes to live in the darkness.

Learning the Lingo

adaptation: The process by which an organism develops traits to help it survive in its habitat or environment. For example, the polar bear has developed white fur that helps hide it from its prey when hunting in the snowy Arctic regions.

diurnal: Animals that prefer to be active during the day. Your pet dog or the squirrels in your park are diurnal.

echolocation: Some animals can gain awareness of their surroundings and prey by making short, high-pitched sounds and listening for how they bounce back. Animals that use echolocation include bats, whales, dolphins, and some birds.

nocturnal: Animals that are active at night. Examples of nocturnal animals are badgers, bats, kangaroos, owls, scorpions, skunks, and wolves.

rhodopsin: The chemical in our eyes that builds up in the darkness and helps us see at night.

Materials

- Bandanna

Plan of Attack

NIGHT VISION: We have a chemical in our eyes, called *rhodopsin*, which helps us see at night. There is more of this chemical activated in our eyes when the light is very low. That's why it can be uncomfortable to go from a very dark room to a very light or sunny room. The rhodopsin is "burned off" by the sunlight and your eyes need time to adjust to the changing light. Conversely, your eyes also need time to adjust to low-light conditions and build up some rhodopsin to be able to see. Rhodopsin has to connect to the rods in your eyes to activate. Scientists believe that owls have 100 times more rods in their eyes than humans. This is one of the reasons that owls can see so well at night. It is said that owls can spot a mouse using the light given off by just one candle almost a half of a mile away!

It takes about 20 minutes in low light conditions to have your full night vision activated. Let's do a demonstration to show you how it works:

1. Sit in a dark room at night for about 20 minutes. No TV, no computer, no light. Maybe you can just sit back and listen to some music. Make sure it is dark throughout your whole house.

2. Now, walk in darkness to your bathroom. It should be fairly easy because your eyes have activated your night vision by building up their rhodopsin.

3. Next, shut your left eye completely and cover it with your hand. Your goal is for no light to make it in. Now, turn the light in the bathroom on for 10 to 20 seconds while keeping your right eye open (and still covering and closing your left). Turn the light off. You have now "burned off" the rhodopsin from your right eye.

4. Walk around your dark house now with both eyes open and compare the vision in your two eyes. You will notice how much better your left eye can see compared to your right. This is because of rhodopsin!

ECHOLOCATION: How can bats see in total darkness and find insects to pluck out of the air and eat? The answer is echolocation. Think about it like this: if you go to a rock canyon and yell out, the noise will bounce around the rock walls and echo back to you. Bats find their food using the same principle. Bats send out tiny, high-pitched sounds that are echoed back to them. Some whales and dolphins also use echolocation to navigate the vast ocean and hunt for food.

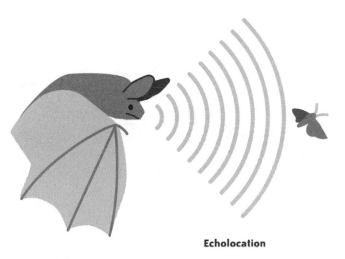

Echolocation

These sounds are so high-pitched that humans can't hear them. When these sounds get interrupted (by an insect for example) the bat's brain can pinpoint where the insect is and attack. This isn't even something the bat has to consciously think about. It's the same as you or I seeing or hearing; they just do it. In this activity you play a game demonstrating echolocation.

1. You'll need another person and a bandanna. Find a 10-foot-by-10-foot area to play in. It's important to stay within the established area. One person will be the bat and the other person will be the insect.

2. Next, the *bat* will tie the bandanna around his eyes so he can't see. The blind bat is trying to tag the insect in the game area. While the bat can't see, he can pretend to send out echoes by clapping his hands once. When the bat claps, the insect *must* clap her hands in response. This is demonstrating echolocation. As the bat hears the clap, he will be able to figure out where the insect is and will try to tag her.

3. The game ends when the bat tags the insect. Now switch!

Take It to the Max!

Sometimes the best ideas come from nature. A huge, multibillion-dollar nuclear submarine uses technology very similar to a bat's echolocation called SONAR to find enemy ships. Find out the similarities and differences between the echolocation technique of a bat and the SONAR technology of a navy sub.

CAUSTIC CONSEQUENCES: PH-INDING OUT ABOUT YOUR WATER

Content Focus: Biology
Primary Skills Focus: Interpreting Data

Mission Objective: Soak in some knowledge about water and air pollution by finding out the acidity of water in your home and area.

Can you imagine a time when almost all the natural water around us was clean? It's pretty hard to imagine nowadays, but that was what it was like in North America for hundreds of thousands of years. Our lakes and rivers began becoming polluted in the 1800s when big manufacturing companies started producing things like tires, toothpaste, and other everyday items, dumping the waste products in the waterways after production.

Not only did they dump waste into the lakes and rivers, but some of their huge smokestacks sent thousands of pounds of polluted gas into the atmosphere. Today there are laws to limit the pollution, but for a long time there weren't any. Did you know that there was even a river that was so polluted it caught on fire? It's true; in 1969 the Cuyahoga River in Ohio had so much oil in it that it actually burst into flames. Obviously, this pollution is not good for the environment.

As you learned in the water cycle learning activity, there is a constant cycle of evaporation and precipitation happening all the time. All this means is that water on the surface of the Earth heats up and changes from a liquid to a vapor. These vaporous water molecules come together in the atmosphere to become clouds. These clouds then give us (and our crops) the rainwater we need to survive. But what if the air was polluted so badly that the evaporated water (clouds) became *infected* with pollution? Then, the rain that was falling from the sky would be contaminated. We call that acid rain. Acid rain can hurt the soil, plants, and trees, and can even damage cars and statues. In this activity you are going to become an ecologist and decide how acidic your local water is.

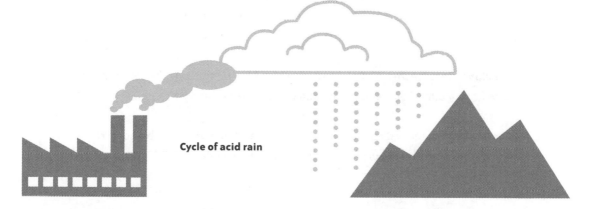

Cycle of acid rain

Learning the Lingo

acid rain: When pollution in the air mixes with clouds and makes the rainwater polluted.

litmus paper: Specially treated strips of paper that measure pH levels.

pH: A measurement of the concentration of hydrogen ions in a substance. pH can tell us how acidic a substance is.

pollution: The contamination of the environment, oftentimes by harmful substances.

Materials

- Head of red cabbage
- Blender
- Water
- Pot
- Medium-sized bowl
- 5–10 strips of white paper, 1 inch by 4 inches
- 3 small bowls containing ¼ cup each of three substances to test: vinegar, water, and window cleaner

Plan of Attack

In this mission you determine the pH (acidity) level of common household liquids and a body of water near your home. pH measures the concentration of hydrogen ions in a substance. The pH scale goes from 0 to 14:

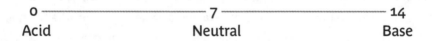

0	7	14
Acid	Neutral	Base

Acidic substances are things like hydrochloric acid, battery acid, vinegar, and lemons. Basic substances include ammonia and bleach. Obviously, neither end of this scale would be good for aquatic organisms living in your ponds or rivers. Some aquatic organisms can live only in specific pH ranges. For example, the ideal range for rainbow trout is a pH of 6.5 to 8.0. By making homemade litmus paper, you will be able to test the pH level of water in your area and see if aquatic life in your neighborhood is at risk.

✳ **Very Important!** *Because this mission involves making hot items using the stove or microwave, you need to have a parent or responsible adult do this activity with you.*

1. Cut off ¼ to ⅓ of the red cabbage from the head and place it in the blender. You are looking for the most purple-colored parts of the vegetable.

2. Add just a small amount (no more than 1 cup) of water and blend. You want to get it to a pasty, soupy consistency.

3. Next, pour this purplish goop into the pot and bring to a boil on the stove. Then reduce the heat and simmer for about 5 minutes.

4. After the mixture has cooled a bit, transfer it to a bowl.

5. Submerge the strips of paper into the mixture. After they have absorbed much of the cabbage juice—you'll be able to tell because they will turn purple—take them out and let them dry. As they dry they will turn blue. You have now made homemade litmus paper!

6. Test your three liquid substances to find out if they are acidic, neutral, or basic by dipping a strip into each. The color of the litmus paper will tell you: If the strip turns pink/light purple, the substance is acidic. If the strip stays the same blue, it is neutral. If it takes on a yellowy/greenish hue, it is basic. Try it out on vinegar (acidic), tap water (hopefully neutral), and window cleaner (basic) to make sure it works.

7. Last, visit some local bodies of water with an adult. These could include a lake, stream, pond, or river. Find out if each body of water is acidic, basic, or neutral. How do you think this could influence the aquatic life below the surface?

Take It to the Max!

You now understand how important the role of pollution is in the quality of the water all around you. One of the major pollutants in the air comes from burning coal that gives off a substance called *sulfur dioxide*. Sulfur dioxide makes up a major portion of acid rain. Learn about the controversy surrounding coal in the United States.

HOW THE GILLS GET THEIR FILL: ABSORBING OXYGEN AS A FISH

Content Area: Biology
Primary Skills Focus: Investigating and Classifying

Mission Objective: Splash into the science of how fish take in oxygen through their gills. Then, see this firsthand by dissecting a fish and examining its anatomy.

Have you ever wondered why you have to hold your breath when you are swimming? Have you ever wondered how fish can swim without ever having to come up for air? You are about to become a marine biologist learning how fish use the water around them to breathe. Along the way you will also get a chance to learn about amazing scientific principles of how oxygen is used by you to do something you can't live without—breathing.

Learning the Lingo

diffusion: Movement of molecules (remember oxygen can be used to make many different molecules) from an area of high concentration to an area of lower concentration. Think of diffusion as what happens when people leave a really crowded room to move into a less crowded room until both rooms have an equal amount of people. Gases are freely moving and can then diffuse, or move, into other substances, like oxygen gas diffusing into water.

gas: A state of matter that is different than a solid or liquid. Gases can expand and contract with pressure and temperature. Gases have no shape of their own, they just adjust to the shape of their container.

gills: A respiratory organ in many animals that live underwater. Gills are the organs that let fish breathe.

lungs: A respiratory organ in many animals that live on land. Lungs are the organs that let humans breathe.

oxygen: An element found in nature, symbolized by the letter O. It can combine with other elements to be part of compounds like water. In its free, or natural, form it is a colorless, odorless gas. This is the gas form that can be used for breathing.

Materials

- 1 whole fish (from your local fish market or grocery store) or, alternatively, a good picture of a fish's anatomy from a textbook or the Internet
- Newspaper
- Disposable gloves

- Safety goggles
- Paperclip (unwound, to be used as a probe)

Plan of Attack

Even after learning the lingo, you probably still have many questions. Both humans and fish use oxygen to breathe, and we both need oxygen from the environment for energy to live.

With the new information you have just learned, and an exciting chance to see the anatomy of a fish up close, you will learn how these amazing animals get their oxygen to live. You will then learn how this is both different from and in some ways similar to the way humans breathe.

1. At your local grocery store or fish market, talk to the person in charge of the seafood counter. Explain that you are doing a science project on the way fish take in oxygen from the water, and that you are interested in a whole fish (or fish head with the gills still in place). It does not matter what type of fish it is.

2. Place the fish in a bag surrounded by ice to keep it cold, then refrigerate until you are ready to use. Otherwise the fish may spoil and may start to smell bad.

    If you cannot get a fish from a store don't worry. You can get a picture of the anatomy of any fish from your local library (ask your librarian) or from the Internet. You can still learn everything you need from looking at detailed pictures closely.

3. Once you get the fish home, spread newspaper down on a kitchen table or flat surface and lay the fish on top.

4. Wear plastic gloves to handle the fish, and make sure to wear protection for your eyes.

The Dissection:

5. First inspect some of the anatomy of the fish. Identify a) the mouth, b) the eyes, c) the operculum (a bony flap that covers and protects the gills, usually located somewhere behind the eye), d) the gills (located underneath the operculum). Look closely at these areas.

6. Use the unwound paperclip to probe the area inside the mouth. Can you see the paperclip behind the operculum?

7. Push the paperclip tip behind the operculum through the gills. Where is the end of the probe after it goes through the gills?

8. You can see the connection between the fish's mouth, gills, and the outside world by passing your probe through the mouth and gills.

9. Examine the gills. Does it look like water can pass through or around the gills, or are the gills completely solid?

10. Look for the nostrils on the fish. Does it have them?

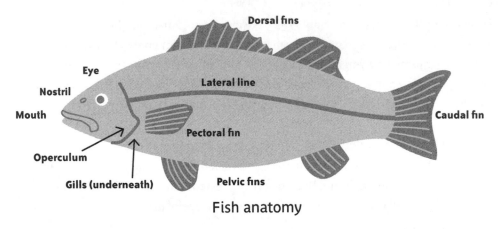

Fish anatomy

Does it look like there is a connection between the mouth and the gills? You were right, there is!

Fish are able to breathe by taking water in through their mouth and pushing it through their gills back outside of their body. The process is kind of like how humans breathe air in and out through our noses and mouths. So it makes sense that there is a connection between the fish's mouth, its gills, and the outside of its body.

But that doesn't explain how the fish get the oxygen out of the water and into their bodies. Remember that oxygen is found in many substances around us. Oxygen is found in the air we breathe, in the soil, and in the water. Oxygen is in two different forms in the water. Oxygen is used to make up the liquid, as in H2O, and "extra" oxygen is in the same water in the form of oxygen gas dissolved in liquid. It is the oxygen gas inside of the water that the fish uses to breathe.

Since there is oxygen gas in the water, and the water goes in the fish's mouth, through the gills, and out the fish's body, how does the oxygen gas get transferred inside the fish for use as energy? The gills of a fish are a membranous, leaf-like structure behind the head of the fish. Inside of the membranes (or special skin) of the gills are small capillaries, which are small blood vessels. Oxygen from the water is absorbed through these tiny blood vessels and becomes part of the blood that is sent to different parts of the fish to be used as energy.

Remember the definition of diffusion? Well, diffusion is the way oxygen goes from water to the bloodstream through the membrane of the gills. There is less oxygen in the blood vessels going through the gills than there is in the water, so oxygen moves into the blood. At the same time carbon dioxide (which is a waste product the fish doesn't need) gets diffused back into the water. This constantly happens as a fish takes in water through its mouth and pushes it out through its gills. That is how they breathe underwater.

So why can't humans do that too? Our lungs can only use the oxygen that is in air for breathing. Our lungs use oxygen from air, and take that oxygen into our blood, just like the fish. The difference is that they get oxygen from water and we get the oxygen from air.

Take It to the Max!

You now know a little about how water is taken in by fish to get oxygen that is then used for energy, but did you see that fish do indeed have nostrils? What do you think they use their nostrils for? Research and find out.

SAY WHAT? THE SCIENCE OF SOUND

Content Area: Biology
Primary Skills Focus: Exploring Connections

Mission Objective: Investigate how the human body can physically detect sound and then complete a hands-on experiment demonstrating the principles of sound waves.

Ready or not, "hear" it comes! Have you ever wondered how those beautiful sounds travel from a violin, guitar, or other instrument to your ears? Have you ever had to cover your ears, but you thought you could feel the sound going into your head? You are about to uncover an interesting world of sound, and find out about how your body hears the sound.

See how the science of sound comes alive by unlocking the mystery of your ears and making your own music.

Learning the Lingo

frequency: A measurement of the speed or time between top points and bottom points of the wave. The top is called the *peak* and the bottom is called the *trough*. Different frequency sound waves give off different sounds. But not all frequencies can be audible, or heard, by humans.

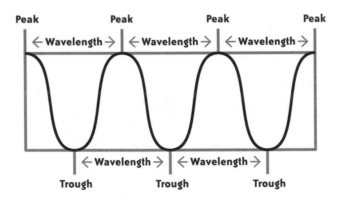

perception of sound: What sound frequencies can be heard by a living creature? Generally, humans can only perceive, or hear, sounds from a certain range of frequencies. Other living creatures, like dogs or bats, can hear different frequencies than humans.

sound waves or pressure waves: A sound wave is the pattern of how energy changes as it moves or travels through a substance. This substance could be air, liquid, or even solid. Why is it called a wave? When something vibrates, the energy that is released as a sound has a pattern. The specific patterns of sounds that are released by vibration are in a waveform. Sound waves have characteristics based on how fast the waves travel and how tall or short the waves are.

vibration: A specific movement, which is mechanical in nature, that happens when a solid or flexible object moves back and forth from its normal position. For example, a drum vibrates when you hit it with a drumstick. The movement happens when the drum is hit, and it vibrates the top of the drum and creates sound.

Materials

Sound of Water

- Small bowl
- Teaspoon
- Glass (preferably a wine glass or fluted glass)
- Several cups of water

Rubber Band Guitar

- Small (shoebox size) cardboard box
- Safety scissors
- Rubber bands (at least 6 of different thicknesses)
- 12 push pins

Plan of Attack

What is sound? It seems like an easy question, doesn't it? You hear sounds every day—you probably hear sounds all around you right now—yet sound is not that easy to define. Sound comes from vibrations transmitted through the air (or liquid or gas). The sound vibrations travel through the air in waves. These waves can be thought of just like waves of the ocean—they have a peak and a valley, or top and bottom.

Sound waves can travel at different frequencies, which can be thought of as how fast the waves are making these ups and downs, or peaks and valleys. The more peaks and valleys, the higher the frequency. Frequencies can be measured and used to understand different sounds. Frequencies can be measured in a unit called *hertz*.

You might be wondering, can we see these sound waves like the waves on the beach? Yes and no. Sound waves can travel through different things like air, liquid, or solids. Sometimes you will be able to see the vibration associated with the sound wave, like when you see a guitar string move back and forth. But, depending on the frequency, we will not necessarily be able to see the waves, or vibrations, that make other sounds. In fact there are some frequencies that we are not able to hear either.

Why can't we hear all frequencies? It is because the anatomy of our ear, including the bones and nerves, lets us hear only certain frequencies. Humans, in general, can hear the same set of frequencies, but other living things may hear other frequencies of sound based on their anatomy. Have you ever wondered why humans cannot hear a dog whistle? It is because we do not hear that frequency.

Sound waves travel through the air and go through your ear canal to your eardrum. The sound waves vibrate your eardrum and move bones in your ear. These bones move and transmit the sound to the nerve that controls hearing, which takes the sound to your brain to process it. Your brain can tell what the sound is based on many things, including the frequency.

Remember different sounds have different characteristics, but they all provide vibrations that give off sound waves. You are about to see how changing the properties of materials can change the way they vibrate, giving off different sounds or sound waves. Put what you have learned to use by making your own sound waves with these different materials.

#1 SOUND OF WATER

1. Fill up the small bowl halfway with water.

2. Fill the teaspoon with water and drop a few drops of water into the bowl.

3. Note the sound the drops of water make when hitting the water in the bowl.

4. Can you see the "waves" that are made when the drops of water from the spoon hit the surface of the water?

5. Now fill the wine glass with water and pour a steady stream of water into the bowl.

6. Note the sound the steady stream of water made when hitting the water in the bowl.

7. Fill your wineglass almost to the top with water. Tap the side of the glass gently with your teaspoon. Note the sound or pitch this makes.

8. Repeat this with the glass half filled with water, and then ¼ filled with water. Note the sound or pitch made with different levels of water.

This activity is a good way to understand that vibrations make sound. The water hitting against other water made a vibration and made sound waves. The drops of water made a different frequency of sound compared to the steady stream, giving you a different sound. If you looked closely, you were also able to see waves move through the water by looking at the ripples. When the glass of water is tapped by the spoon, this vibrates the glass. The sound wave travels through the water as well, and makes different sounds based on how much water is in the glass.

Next you will see how rubber bands can be stretched to different lengths and moved to vibrate, giving different frequencies of sound.

#2 RUBBER BAND GUITAR

1. Using safety scissors, cut a hole approximately 6 inches in diameter in the middle of the top of the cardboard box. Place the top back on the box.

2. Cut the rubber bands (to create one straight string of rubber) and stretch them across the hole to make a line of at least six "strings" of different thickness. Keep the rubber bands in place by inserting push pins through the bands.

3. Pluck each string using your finger.

4. Note that different string thicknesses make different sounds. This is because the rubber bands create different frequencies of sound based on the size and tension of each.

5. Watch the vibrations as each rubber band is plucked. The vibrating rubber bands are creating invisible sound waves.

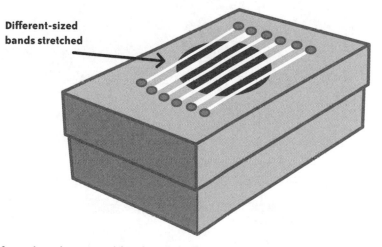

Different-sized bands stretched

You have heard sound waves from the vibrating rubber bands and now understand how easy and complex things like music and hearing can be.

Take It to the Max!

Have you ever felt your ears "pop" when you were going up a hill or riding in a plane? This sensation has to do with pressure in your middle ear space. Learn about what controls the amount of pressure in your middle ear.

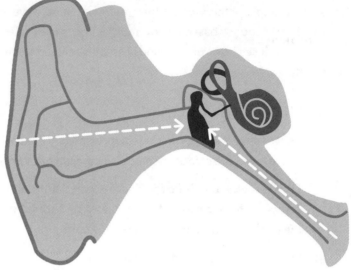

FUN GUY OR FUNGI? THE WORLD OF YEASTS AND MOLDS

Content Area: Biology
Primary Skills Focus: Measuring and Observing

Mission Objective: Uncover the basics of fungus, yeasts, and molds and then use this knowledge of yeasts to make tasty pizza dough.

Have you ever seen a piece of food in your refrigerator or fruit bowl that has been there too long and has a small green or black fuzzy patch on it? You may have been told that your food had fungus growing on it and it wasn't safe to eat anymore. Not only was it not safe for you, but it looks gross too. But, did you know that there are different types of fungi, and they are literally all around you? Sometimes the fungi are so small that you can't even see them without a microscope. You may be surprised to find out that fungi have been used to make many different products, from detergents to soy sauce.

You will soon see how different types of fungi, including yeasts and molds, make up the world around you, including the food you eat. You can even try using your new fungi friends to make some food of your own.

Learning the Lingo

fungus: A group of living organisms, different from animals, plants, and bacteria. Fungi, which are more than one fungus, can be made up of one cell (unicellular) or many cells (multicellular). This group of organisms includes microorganisms like yeast or mold, and the more well-known mushrooms.

mold: A type of fungus that is multicellular (more than one cell) and grows in a form of tubular branches that are known as *hyphae* (pronounced HIGH-fay). Although molds can cause disease and food spoilage, they have also been used for making different medicines. Molds can also be used in making cheese, breads, and soy sauce.

mycology: The branch of biology that is concerned with the study of fungi. If you want to study fungus, you can become a mycologist.

penicillin: A group of medicines that are antibiotics (that help kill bacteria), which were derived from the fungus penicillium.

yeast: A type of single-celled fungus. There are different types of yeast; the most common type of yeast used by humans is called *Saccharomyces cerevisiae*. Its more common name (and easier to say name) is baker's yeast, and it is used in baking different types of bread.

Materials

- Large mixing bowl
- 1 cup warm water
- 1 tablespoon sugar
- 2¼ teaspoons active dry yeast
- 1 teaspoon salt
- 3½ tablespoons olive oil
- 2½ cups all-purpose flour
- Rolling pin
- Pizza pan
- Favorite pizza toppings
- Pastry brush

Plan of Attack

Fungi are interesting organisms when compared to animals, plants, and bacteria. Scientists believe that there are over 1.5 million different species, or types, of fungi. Fungi play a very important role in the cycle of life on our planet by taking part in decomposition and in the exchange of nutrients.

Two different types of fungi are yeasts and molds. Molds are made up of more than one cell, have a branching pattern that looks like filaments, and form colonies (a colony is a grouping of mold cells). Molds reproduce through small spores. The goal of the spores is to travel to an area where they can live comfortably. Mold spores can live for a long time floating in the air and can survive extreme temperatures. Depending on the type of mold and where it grows, it can be harmful or helpful to humans. Remember that one of the most important medicines, penicillin, is synthesized by mold.

Yeasts are another type of fungi. Yeasts are a single-celled type of fungus that reproduces by budding. Yeast has been used for thousands of years to make food items like bread and wine. Some types of yeasts (just like molds) can cause an infection in your body if your immune system is too weak to fight them off.

Fungi live in every continent in the world. Fungi absorb nutrients from the environment around them. Fungi get their energy from dead, decaying organisms or they live off another living organism's nutrients. This does not necessarily hurt the other organism; sometimes they live like a team. In the case of yeast, one of the ways it obtains energy is by using the sugars found in or on another source. The yeast will take the sugar in and release carbon dioxide gas. This gas usually goes up into the air, but in certain instances this gas gets trapped. This is what happens when we make certain types of breads or doughs that rise. These breads have an airy texture with bubbles in the dough. This is a perfect example of people using yeast for a good purpose. Now it is time for you to see the yeast in action when you make your own fluffy, rising pizza dough.

✳ *Very Important!* *Because this recipe involves boiling water, you need to have a parent or responsible adult do this activity with you.*

1. Preheat your oven to 425 degrees Fahrenheit.

2. In a large mixing bowl mix your water, sugar, and yeast together. Make sure the water is between 105 and 115 degrees Fahrenheit.

3. Remember that yeast is a living organism and your goal is for it to use the sugar and release carbon dioxide to make fluffy pizza dough that rises. Yeast like a certain temperature of water, so try not to have your water too cold or hot. Too much colder and your dough will become sticky, too much hotter and the yeast will get too hot and die.

4. After your yeast, water, and sugar are well mixed, add salt and olive oil. Keep ½ tablespoon of the oil aside to brush on the crust over your pizza after you put the toppings on.

5. Now your mixture has all the ingredients except the flour. Add the flour and mix it in to make a nice dough. If the dough is too sticky, add small amounts of flour until the dough does not stick to your hands. If it is too dry, you can add a small amount of water.

6. Make your dough into a ball and note its size. Leave the dough in your bowl for 10 to 12 minutes to let it rise, or let the yeast produce carbon dioxide gas, which will make the dough fluffy. During this time it should grow at least ½ times larger.

7. Roll or hand flatten the dough on a pizza pan and put on your favorite pizza toppings (depending on the size of the pizza you want to make, you should have enough dough for one very large or two medium pizzas).

8. Brush some of your leftover oil around the edges to make it become golden brown after baking.

9. Bake for 15 to 20 minutes, and enjoy your pizza!

Now that you are enjoying your pizza, try not to forget that yeast, a living organism, helped to make this treat for you. The rising dough and the bubbles you saw when you mixed the yeast and water were from that special type of fungi that produces carbon dioxide gas when making energy. Now that you understand the amazing properties of yeasts, molds, and fungi, go ahead and make it a double dose of fungi by adding some mushrooms to your next pizza.

Take It to the Max!

The cell walls of fungi are made with a substance called *chitin*. Is chitin used for any special purposes by humans? Find out what chitin is and what chitin is useful for.

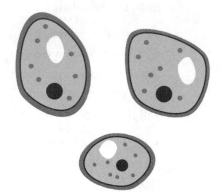

THE ROTTEN TRUTH ABOUT YOUR TEETH

Content Focus: Biology
Primary Skills Focus: Exploring Connections

Mission Objective: Be amazed by tooth care techniques throughout history and then conduct an experiment that simulates tooth decay due to increased sugar exposure.

There is a battle going on in your mouth right now! While we need food to live, the act of chewing our food leaves tiny bits of food on our teeth that can cause cavities. For as long as humans have existed we have been trying to find a way to get all the food and nourishment we need while also keeping our teeth healthy enough to use. The way we take care of our teeth today is pretty different than how people have cared for their teeth throughout history.

While most of us brush, floss, and rinse our teeth to keep them as clean and white as possible, most people throughout history had brown teeth. The products simply weren't available to keep their teeth white. Ancient Chinese would take the bristles (thick hairs) of cold-climate pigs or horses to use for toothbrush bristles. In some Muslim countries people would chew on a stick called a *miswak* to keep their teeth clean. This twig not only helped scrape away material from teeth but also killed bacteria. A study found that mints laced with miswak were 20 times more effective than mints that were not. Modern toothbrushes were not manufactured until the late 1800s, but even then people didn't brush their teeth that often. It was actually the army making soldiers brush their teeth during World War II that led to increased brushing habits in our country.

Ill-cared-for teeth can rot and even fall out. In the past people had to be pretty creative in replacing their rotted teeth. There were reports of grave robbing, with the looters selling the corpses' teeth! Other desperate souls would pull out their own teeth to sell. Some would tie an animal's tooth tightly to a tooth still in place. Legend has it that George Washington had wooden dentures (fake teeth). This is untrue. Scientists have discovered that his dentures were made of gold, ivory, lead (metal), human teeth, and horse or donkey teeth. Today dentures are made of acrylic or plastics. They are much stronger than other materials and can look exactly like real teeth. The lesson of this mission is to take care of your teeth; you only get one set. In this activity you will see how easy it is for substances to eat away at your teeth.

Learning the Lingo

calcium: A mineral that is the building block for strong bones and teeth. Milk, spinach, and broccoli are all great sources of calcium for your body.

denture: Dentures are fake teeth. In the past, people made dentures out of metal, animal teeth, and human teeth. Nowadays dentures are made out of acrylics or high-strength plastics.

fluoride: Fluoride is a chemical that can help slow or stop tooth decay. Your dentist gives you fluoride treatments, and many towns and cities put fluoride in the water supply to help their citizens' teeth.

plaque: Plaque is your teeth's enemy. When we eat certain foods bacteria is left behind on our teeth. If these bacteria aren't removed (through brushing or flossing) it can harden on our teeth into plaque. Plaque buildup can cause tooth decay and other oral problems.

Materials

- 4 small bowls
- 1 cup each of cola, orange juice, vinegar, and water
- 4 white hard-boiled eggs
- Toothbrush

Plan of Attack

Your teeth are made up of calcium, among other things. Calcium is an element that helps give your teeth and bones strength and structure. There is a lot of calcium in milk (that's why your parents may have you drink milk with your dinner). While calcium is strong, some substances can break it down or stain it. In this experiment you are going to pretend the eggshells are your teeth (there is a lot of calcium in eggshells also). Let's see what happens when everyday food and drinks are left on your teeth.

✳ ***Very Important!*** *Because this recipe involves boiling water, you need to have a parent or responsible adult do this activity with you.*

1. Hard-boil 4 eggs with an adult (you may want to boil a couple extra in case of accidents).

2. Pour one cup of each of the following liquids into its own separate bowl: cola, orange juice, vinegar, and water.

3. Submerge 1 egg in each bowl overnight. Make a hypothesis (your best educated guess) as to which liquid will hurt the "teeth" the most.

4. Observe the effects of the liquids on the eggshells the next day. Some substances will dissolve calcium. Others will make it rough and bumpy or just stain.

5. Try to clean the eggs with the toothbrush. Pretty hard, huh?

What happened to the eggs will happen to your teeth if you don't brush them. The plaque (the bacteria that can form and harden on your teeth) will destroy the strength of your teeth if it's not removed. That's why it is so important to brush and floss every day.

Take It to the Max!

Animals don't brush their teeth, but some of them have white, healthy teeth. Why? Find out how animals help keep their teeth white and healthy. Hint: It relates to our discussion of the miswak stick.

ACTIVITIES LIST BY PRIMARY SKILLS FOCUS

CREATIVE EXPRESSION

Take Shelter, There's a Brainstorm Rolling In! The Starting Point of Creative Writing

Wizard of Words: Metaphors and Similes

안녕하세! World Wise: Languages Around the Globe

How to Sign What's on Your Mind: Learning Sign Language

DESIGN AND MODEL

Shoot! Mine Didn't Open: The Science of Parachutes

Spanning the Ages: The Physics of Bridges

Taking Off! The Science of Flight

How Does That Boat Float? Water Displacement and Buoyancy

EXPLORING CONNECTIONS

Molecules, Atoms, and Peanut Brittle: How Good Chemistry Can Taste

The Silent Buildup: Cholesterol, Fats, and Oil

Are You a Mosquito Magnet? To Learn and Protect

Marking Its Way Through History: The Story of Ink

Getting the Dirt on Soil Pollution

Hey Fellow, Why's That Pulp Yellow? The Science of Antique Paper

Globalization: How the World Is Connected

When Nighttime Is the Right Time: Nocturnal Adaptations

Say What? The Science of Sound

The Rotten Truth About Your Teeth

HISTORICAL INQUIRY

Go West! The American Pioneer

The Songs of the Wind: Native American Religious Tradition

Rock the Vote by "Rocking the Boat"?

This Land Is My Land, This Land Is Your Land: The Black Hills Treaty

The Fabric of America: Immigration

INTERPRETING DATA

Is a Penny Saved Really a Penny Earned? Lessons in Investment

Calorie Tracker: Intake Verus Output

Something Borrowed, Something New: How Credit Works

Caustic Consequences: pH-inding Out About Your Water

INVESTIGATING AND CLASSIFYING

The Original Solar Panel: How Leaves Harness Energy

The Sleuth of Truth: A Literary Treasure Hunt

Aahh. . . The Air We Breathe

Democracy! What's Your Vote?

How Much of the Story Are You Getting? Bias in the Media

How the Gills Get their Fill: Absorbing Oxygen as a Fish

MEASURING AND OBSERVING

The Great Ice Enigma: Conservation of Mass and the Science of Volume

Peter Piper Picked a Peck of Cucumbers? Food Preservation Then and Now

The Bright Side of Decomposition: Plants, Pressure, and Oil

Don't Move—You're in Quicksand!

More Than Just a Pretty Taste: Crystals

Nothing New Under the Sun: The Beauty of the Water Cycle

Fun Guy or Fungi? The World of Yeasts and Molds